the FUN-duh-mental LEADER

the **FUN-duh-mental**
LEADER

10 **FUNDAMENTAL THINGS TO KNOW**
AboutRunning a Non-Profit Organization

Rita McCoy

SOUND OFF PUBLISHING

The Fun-duh-mental Leader: 10 Fundamental Things to Know about Running a Non-Profit Organization

Published by Sound Off Publishing
Kissimmee, FL

ISBN: 978-0-9993068-0-2

Library of Congress Control Number: 2017912561

Non-Profit / Management & Leadership

QUANTITY PURCHASES: Schools, companies, professional groups, clubs, and other organizations may qualify for special terms when ordering quantities of this title. For information, email soundoffpublishing@gmail.com.

Contents

Chapter 7 – Marketing and Public Relations

Acknowledgments

I WOULD LIKE TO acknowledge and thank the following people who inspired me to complete this book: My husband Anthony McCoy for his intellectual insights surrounding this book. My sister Tamara Smith Roldan for her continuous encouragement and support throughout the entire process. Polly Letofsky for her guidance and resources leading to the completion of the project. And Melanie Mulhall for her dynamic editorial skills.

I am most grateful to each of you. Thank you so much.

Introduction

A S A FORMER EXECUTIVE director, I want to share my personal experience of being a leader. It is a dynamic and influential position that is highly rewarding, yet filled with challenges. After years of management experience, when I was given my first opportunity to be an executive-in-charge of an organization, the first thing I thought about was that being an influential leader in charge of an organization would be ecstatically *fun*. I enthusiastically and joyfully accepted the offer because I knew I could make a difference in people's lives. I envisioned hard work, long days, and incredible challenges.

While writing this book, I anticipated helping the executive director, CEO, or chairperson of a nonprofit organization. But then I was approached by an individual who asked about others working for nonprofits who might be thrown into leadership roles. Could the information be beneficial to them? The answer is yes. Anyone working for a small-to-medium-size nonprofit and asked to run operations can benefit from what I have learned throughout my years serving as a nonprofit executive director.

Regardless of your title, if you are working for a nonprofit and you are placed in a leadership role or you become the person in charge of running the day-to-day operations of the organization, this book can benefit you. It will help you think about the process, procedures, and fundraising avenues to sustain the organization. As a leader, you may be responsible for strategic planning, fundraising, direction, and implementation. You may be the hiring and firing manager. If you are the person who fills the position as leader, you may wonder what is required of you.

I was looking forward to having fun making a difference and making the position an enjoyable and memorable experience, but I would later find that fun is a matter of choice and that being a leader of a nonprofit came with overwhelming mental challenges, responsibilities, and demands I never anticipated. Any new or aspiring leader should know that the job requirements may create enormous pressure with high anxiety and mental distress. But there are methods, techniques, and systems that can be put in place to lessen the strain. I am going to share some strategies on how to put the *fun*-duh-mental aspects of being an executive leader to work.

THE FUN-DUH-MENTAL LEADER

The reason I make *fun* stand out is because somewhere along the way, that's exactly what you should be having. Being a leader should be fun, a challenge at times, yet filled with great rewards. It is your passion that drives the mission behind great causes. Your job is to help those in need, to be a beacon of hope. You bring about change in people's lives and improve their qualities of life. You are a champion helping to make systemic and social change. All of that is fulfilling and energizing. When the elements of your job become overpowering, it's time to stop and have some fun.

The "duh" in the middle of fun-duh-mental expresses the fact that you do not know everything, so stop pretending. Amazingly, many people think that the lead mind of the organization should know everything, have the answer to every question, and be able to solve every problem. But just because you wear the executive title does not mean you have all the answers. Essentially, that's why you hire staff and consultants, recruit volunteers and interns, and work closely with the board of directors. Let them provide expertise in their respective areas.

The "mental" in fun-duh-mental represents the mental anguish, agony, stress, fatigue, and burnout inherent in the leadership position. Yes, burnout. The "mental" part is what I want to help you tackle because the position can lead to pure exhaustion unless you are careful and look for the warning signs. Instead of fearing the unknown territory you are about to enter, let this be a time to discover the true potential that lies within you.

As a first-time leader, there are some things you know because of the education, experience, talents, skills, and abilities you bring to the new position. If you did not possess those things, the board of directors or trustees would not have chosen you to lead. You were chosen, and now you must prove to those who trust you exactly what you are made of, how you got to be where you are, and how you plan on taking the organization to the next level. Welcome aboard!

One thing I learned along the way to executive leadership is that you must always believe in yourself. Always hold on to the belief that you are a dynamic leader. Someone hired you into the leadership position because they believed in you. They appreciated your attributes and abilities far beyond your imagination. They believed you had potential. Now it's your turn to prove it.

The board will identify your strengths, and, yes, they will eventually discover your weaknesses. If they are a good board, they will turn your weaknesses into strengths.

Just know that being a leader—particularly a first-time leader—means that there will be great challenges beyond your skills or personal control to resolve on your own. But don't be dismayed or discouraged because what you are doing is changing lives.

The focus of this book is on the leadership of startup and small nonprofits with small staffs. Why? Because they may not have a business manager, human-resource director, bookkeeper/accountant, IT professional, marketing person, administrative assistant, graphic artist, program manager, development director, special events manager, communications coordinator, or janitor. Of course, all small nonprofit leaders have these positions on their staffing wish lists, but within a small nonprofit, many of these positions are rolled up into one person—known as the leader.

A nonprofit leader of a small organization oversees raising money for a good cause through individuals, corporations, special events and foundation grants. The nonprofit leader's challenges may include a shortage of paid personnel, volunteers who have other commitments, unskilled labor, outdated equipment and computers, inadequate office space, and a lack of systems to retain donors. It takes unwavering determination to be successful as a nonprofit executive.

Nonprofit leaders may not have lavish office environments equipped with the latest technology and IT teams. Some work environments may be unattractive, while others are quite elaborate. Leaders working for nonprofits often secure locations near the clients they serve because proximity is vital to a nonprofit. A nonprofit working with the homeless population may be in a low-income neighborhood instead of an affluent neighborhood. Soup kitchens, safe houses, and urban youth centers are typically located in highly populated urban cities instead of rural areas. Rural area residents may have services provided by local churches or governmental agencies to assist with basic human needs.

Throughout this book you will see that I use "leader" interchangeably with "executive," "executive leader," and "executive-in-charge." The leader of a small nonprofit must meet challenges far beyond his or her control due to the nature of nonprofits. If a big funder is unable to fund one year, the nonprofit could suffer a tremendous decline in revenue that threatens the livelihood of the organization. If a disgruntled employee leaves the organization with great animosity, he or she could destroy donor relations and cause a decline in revenue. Nonprofit leaders have a strong responsibility to the staff, donors, board of directors, volunteers, and program recipients.

All of this can be stressful, but the fun-duh-mental leader strives to engage the board of directors, secure funding, inspire staff and volunteers, stay in compliance, manage marketing and public relations, stay on top of the financials, and otherwise juggle the demands of being a nonprofit leader while keeping a positive, optimistic outlook and having some fun.

Let's get started!

1

Tackling the First Days on the Job

IT'S YOUR FIRST DAY on the job as the executive leader. If you're like me, you may have suffered extreme insomnia the night before your big day. Your mind created every possible scenario of how the first day would look and feel. You even visualized your wardrobe. Would the black suit work better than the light blue blazer? Which one shows more authority? How will you greet your new staff? How will they receive you? Will they respect your judgment? Did you overstate your abilities to perform the job? You anxiously anticipate new doors opening and then it happens—the door swings open.

As I walked through the door on my first day, I knew the first line of business was to get to know my staff. I wanted to meet each person face-to-face, paying close attention to perception, body language, and facial expressions. I would quickly learn from their gestures who to trust and who to watch.

Entering the nonprofit world is stepping into a world where people work hard and are dedicated to a cause. Some are stressed due to heavy workloads with limited human and technical resources. They are kindhearted, compassionate, passionate, mission-driven individuals who believe the work they do makes a difference in the lives of those they serve.

This could be the main reason nonprofit staff return to work day after day. The salary in nonprofit organizations is typically not high, due to limited financial resources. In some cases, the budget supports part-time staff. Since salary is not always the incentive, I knew I had to treat employees with the greatest amount of respect, with hopes that they would return the favor.

After I introduced myself and scheduled my one-on-one time with staff members, I felt it was best to meet with them in their own offices because this was the environment in which they felt most comfortable. With each, I asked general questions about their position, background, and experience to better understand their abilities, skill sets, and interests. I listened carefully. The greatest gift you can give to a member of your staff as you build a relationship with them is to listen to what they are saying. Somewhere in the conversation, you will begin to discover their ambitions, goals, desires, problems, and concerns about the organization.

I wanted to get to know my staff, to study their contributions and use them to the best of their abilities. At the same time, I wanted to listen to them and share ideas about how to best serve the organization and its beneficiaries. I did not want to make drastic personnel changes unless necessary. I reminded myself that everyone was not going to think like me. I embraced diversity and differences in the workplace, knowing that there was strength in that diversity.

CREATING A WORKABLE PLAN

After a month, you will determine what is missing inside the organization, whether it is personnel, equipment, programs, or structure. My first few weeks consisted of meeting the people most valuable to the organization: staff members, board members, funders, and community partners. I met with staff members to begin developing relationships with them, as well as to gauge their strengths and weaknesses, and I met with board members to understand their vision and direction. With funders, I wanted to become familiar with their guidelines and deadlines, and with community partners, I wanted to understand what programs were similar to my organization's programs and what collaborative efforts had been achieved.

You have probably outlined what you intend to accomplish within a ninety-day period. If you haven't, it's a good idea to strategize what you want to accomplish over the next three months. The board of directors will evaluate you on your accomplishments within that span of time. Here is an example of what a ninety-day plan might include.

First Week - Meet the Team
✓ Meet with the staff to gain knowledge about day-to-day operations and protocol.
✓ Meet the key people who can help you better understand the past, present, and future of the organization and who provide internal and external support to the organization. Typically, this may be the founder or veteran board member.
✓ Gather information about the organization from those outside it as well as those within it so you can speak passionately about what they do, why they exist, and who they serve. You will be the spokesperson for the organization to gain financial support.

- ✓ Learn how volunteers contribute their time to the organization.
- ✓ Learn how the programs work. How many programs are there? How many people are served?

Second Week –Financial Overview
- ✓ Determine if there are any grant deadlines approaching.
- ✓ Review financial structure and processes including balance sheet, profit and loss statements, payroll, and bank statements.
- ✓ Know the accounting procedures, payroll, and budgets.
- ✓ Review board strategic plan, initiatives, goals, and fundraising strategy. Review any previous SWOT (Strengths, Weaknesses, Opportunities, and Threats) analysis.
- ✓ Analyze revenue streams; determine grant cycles; know the major donors and priorities. Know what special events drive revenue.
- ✓ Schedule a meeting with the treasurer to better understand any concerns about the budget.
- ✓ Know the deadlines for filing annual registrations with the Secretary of State.
- ✓ Find out about annual audit and 990 deadlines. Understand the 941 and tax consequences.

Third Week – Cultivating Relationships
- ✓ Meet with board members one-on-one to get input on challenges and opportunities.
- ✓ Identify major funders to meet and greet. Meet with corporate donors or sponsors.
- ✓ Start to cultivate relationships with donors.
- ✓ Start scheduling time to meet with your network of business associates and introduce them to the nonprofit.
- ✓ Ensure that a media release has been sent introducing new leadership; if no release exists, create one to send to media.

Fourth Week – Researching Funding Sources

✓ Begin researching and identifying new funding sources/collaborative potential.

✓ Consider next level goals and objectives, for instance, how to serve more people through your programs.

Second Month – Community Connections

✓ Identify community committees, task forces, and boards needed to further the mission and programs.

✓ Leverage community connections.

✓ Begin to identify the talents and skills needed for the board.

Third Month – Media Relations

✓ Increase visibility and exposure of the organization through public relations campaigns and/or cause-related marketing techniques.

✓ Increase media contacts; develop relationships with local media.

✓ Continue to build and cultivate new relationships in the community to increase involvement with the organization.

OFFICE ARRANGEMENT

Within the first month, look at your office surroundings. How do you feel about the furniture arrangement? Everyone has their own preference in office arrangements. Do you prefer your back to face the door or the wall? I rearranged the desk and chairs because I felt awkward facing the wall. I preferred facing outward to give attention to staff, visitors, clients, board members, and stakeholders entering my office. Your staff will value your thoughtfulness if you create a warm, friendly, open-door, welcoming environment. What is your comfort level? Does the chair fit your body well? If not, is there something you can do to make it work better for you? Is the setup ergonomically appropriate? Ensure that you arrange your office to provide the highest level of productivity.

Tips on Office Arrangement

✓ Strategically place your desk in a position to greet guests, staff, board members, program participants, and supporters.

✓ Be approachable. Have an open-door policy. By leaving your door open as much as possible, you will be communicating your intent to be open and transparent.

✓ Take the time to rearrange the desk, file cabinets, bookshelves, and chairs to fit your preference, style, and personality.

✓ Remember that efficiency and effective leadership starts with an organized environment to support an organized mind.

UNDERSTANDING THE JOB

Now that your desk is in the right spot, the phone is where it should be, and the file cabinets frequently used are at arm's length, it is time to really review and analyze the job description. Keep in mind that because you are in charge with no day-by-day agenda, it is your job as executive leader to move the organization forward. To do that, you need a road map or driving instructions, and that's where the job description comes in handy.

Driving the organization's mission requires definite planning. So where do you start? By looking at the job description, I concentrated on activities that best aligned with the board objectives. I would be evaluated by the board on fundraising, financial management, board development, staff recruitment and retention, operations, marketing and communications, office systems, partnerships/

collaborations, programs, special events, security, and all other duties as assigned.

What does "all other duties as assigned" mean? It could imply janitorial services such as snow removal, sweeping front porches, disinfecting kitchens, scrubbing toilets, and picking up trash in the alleys. I know it sounds like I'm joking, but keep in mind that as the person in charge, you are classified as the business owner. If the business district requires business owners to pick up trash and remove snow from sidewalks to avoid being sued, you may need to get off your high horse—or get out of your high heels—and start shoveling. Am I speaking hypothetically? No. I have personal experience with picking up trash and shoveling sidewalks. Being the leader of a nonprofit is both a noble form of employment and a humbling one

While my responsibilities seemed overwhelming, I broke the elements down into manageable sections to take away that daunting feeling. Stressing out early in the game makes no sense. I reviewed the job description and other information provided by staff on fundraising activities and due dates of grants. Since no grants were due for another couple of months, I directed my attention to the next responsibility—financial management.

Each day, I automatically turned my attention to fundraising and financial management because it was the driving force of the organization. I knew I needed to bring money in to run operations. I needed strong financial management to ensure that the payroll, operational bills, and program expenses were paid on time. I wanted to establish a routine, but I quickly learned that each day would be different and there is no such thing as routine.

Tips on Understanding the Job

✓ Accept the fact that no two days are the same because emerging issues can derail your plans.

✓ Take a moment during the first few days and weeks to review and analyze the job description.

✓ Let the job description be your guide to remain focused on what to accomplish.

✓ Remember the board will be evaluating you on how well you perform the elements of your job description. Review it often until the work activities become natural.

GETTING TO KNOW WHO'S WHO

Who do you need to know? One of the most important aspects of the job is building collaborations and partnerships on behalf of the organization. I was given a list of community leaders, collaborative partners, stakeholders, donors, and people in the know. This list was my starting point to cultivate relationships.

The list was two pages long, and the good news was that many of the people I needed to connect with attended the same coalition meetings regularly, allowing me to introduce myself to several people at a time. The only people I could not connect with face-to-face were those individuals living in rural areas, some as far as one hundred miles away. I attended as many meetings as possible in the first couple of months to build those connections.

Tips on Getting to Know Who's Who

✓ Create a list of individuals you should connect with monthly and place them in Outlook, Excel or another database where you can make notes to remember their unique characteristics.

✓ Unless you are an expert in every area of management, you

will need individuals with expertise you can consult with about human resources, operations, and/or IT. Be prepared to reach out to those individuals when you need them.

✓ Connect with the movers and shakers—the people well known in their circles. They may belong to different associations.

✓ Join the chamber of commerce, Rotary, or other local groups to increase your network in the community.

COLLABORATIONS AND PARTNERSHIPS

You should keep track of the people you meet. In the first few months as the executive leader, you will meet a large network of individuals. You never know who you will need in the future for advice, assistance, or funding—especially in the world of nonprofits. Develop connections and devise a system to stay connected on a regular basis.

You can even scan business cards or otherwise add them to your computer system for better tracking. I maintained a binder filled with business cards divided by categories such as business services, consultants, media, potential board, fundraisers, and auction donors. While you reconnect with some people every month, you may connect with others no more often than every six months or so. Be proactive in developing a system to know who to call and when. You should stay connected and start developing business relationships that can create higher short-term and long-term revenue sources for your organization.

I used my e-mail system to add notes on where I met people, what services they offered, and other important information. I coded them in my system by area of expertise. I suspected that six months down the road I might need the products or services of at least some of them, and I was correct.

When I became the leader, the first few months required education in the real world of business operations. Sure, I had a business degree and had used a lot of the teachings throughout my career, but now I oversaw growing and sustaining a twelve-year-old organization. All decisions fell on my shoulders. Now I needed to merge classroom knowledge with real-world challenges and consequences. Who could I connect with?

I immediately scheduled lunch and coffee face-to-face meetings with other executives in my sector to probe their minds on business practices, structure, and organization. The advice I received would prove to be everlasting and invaluable. They highlighted their revenue raising challenges and the importance of staying connected with top funders who helped sustain operations and brought in new funders to support the cause.

From these connections and community leaders, I learned that there will be times when it seems hopeless—virtually impossible, even—to increase revenue year after year, and you must maintain your sense of direction, remember your mission, and drive that mission with great enthusiasm, determination, and perseverance. You should never give up and you should never quit mid-way in reaching the revenue goals you and your board of directors set forth. Of course, that does not mean you can never quit your job. It means that while you are in the higher echelon position, you should not give up. Keep pushing the mission forward with innovative, guided strategies to ensure success.

WORKING WITH LIMITED RESOURCES

How else do you find out about industry standards and best practices? If you are a small nonprofit with limited resources, let's face it, you may have limited expertise in every area. In that case, it is best to connect with people who are familiar with industry standards and best practices to protect yourself and your organization.

For instance, I worked for organizations that had a human resource director responsible for policies and procedures, employee performance, exit interviews, and other human resource functions. To ensure that I complied, I consulted with human resource professionals outside the company over lunch to increase my knowledge about employment laws, workers compensation, and processing benefit claims. With those consultation lessons, I gained the knowledge I needed before dashing forward on disciplinary actions, employee orientation, and employee evaluation.

I also joined the Society of Human Resources Management (SHRM) to receive updates on employment standards, regulations, and legal aspects and joined a statewide nonprofit association for training and information on nonprofit management. Membership into such an association is designed to empower nonprofits, offer workshops and seminars on topics such as organizational effectiveness, how to use social media, working with financial software (like QuickBooks), understanding contracts, grant writing, advocacy, health insurance, donor management databases, board building, growing the nonprofit, technology, and many other subjects. You cannot know everything, but you can learn a lot when you tap into resources like these. And that learning will help you become successful in your leadership role.

Another benefit of nonprofit associations is that you can post job openings through them—including those for volunteer and intern positions.

DEALING WITH INTERRUPTIONS

After being in the position for a few months, you will have familiar-
ized yourself with the routine business operations—from how often
the phone rings to how often people visit your facility and how
many times you order office supplies. And while your formal job
description focuses on fundraising and development, your informal
job description includes things like ensuring that you have enough
copy paper and letterhead to complete the holiday appeal letters.
Remember, you are responsible for anything and everything related
to the organization because you drive the bottom line. You must remain alert to the fact that business operations can be unpredictable,
unplanned, and interrupted.

Let me give you a scenario to demonstrate what I mean. You
walk into the office and no one is there. You are about to print
out a large project, and no one has told you that the printer is out
of paper, and no paper in the office. You get in your car, drive to
the nearest office supply store, and return with paper, which con-
sumes thirty minutes of your valuable time. Then you discover that
the printer is not working. You troubleshoot the situation, get the
printer working, and are just about to print your project when the
phone rings. It is a request for a report that takes you two and half
hours to produce. Afterwards, you return to the printing job, an
appeal letter, put paper in the printer, and print your job. Then you
discover that there are no business envelopes. Twenty appeal letters must go out that day to garner support you desperately need,
so you run back to the office supply store and return thirty minutes
later to print the envelopes.

Of course, the lessons here are: 1) never start a print job without
the necessary supplies, and, more importantly, 2) stuff happens. In
the world of small nonprofits, you may not be able to keep your eye

on every single aspect of the business. You must train your eye to stay on top of most things to save time.

Leadership includes some uncontrollable and unforeseeable work activities. They just cannot be avoided. Sixty percent of your time should be spent on activities related to raising funds and the other forty percent to programs and business operations. In other words, your single biggest activity, the one that drives everything else, is fundraising. The only thing in your workday that will be typical is that you will be bombarded with e-mails. Other than that, there will be no typical day. You will have to keep your focus on your main objectives and become graceful about dancing with interruptions and unforeseen urgencies.

And what about those e-mails? My best advice is that it is up to you to control them, not let them control you. If you receive fifty to one hundred e-mails a day, do not get hung up checking e-mail constantly throughout the day. It is more efficient to check e-mails two or three times a day. That could be first thing in the morning and once in the afternoon or first thing in the morning, after lunch, and before going home. Whatever you do, have a plan or you will be tempted to check e-mails throughout the day.

If you need to get a head start on e-mails daily, check them on your cell phone or tablet before leaving home, not while driving. This way, you will know what to expect before arriving at work and will arrive there safely.

Toss all unwanted e-mails into the trash or filter them out. Create e-mail folders to help you keep the important e-mails organized— one for board e-mails, another for fundraising, and so on. Red flag all urgent e-mails and those with a deadline. Revisit them by the end of the day. Avoid printing out e-mails. If you print them out, you will end up with five-inch piles of e-mails to go through—what I call stacks of anxiety. Go green and eliminate the paper clutter.

I once came into the office to find over one hundred e-mails in my inbox. It took me eight hours to reply, research, track information, follow up on requests, and otherwise deal with them. It was a trap, and I fell into it. Do what you can to avoid unnecessary e-mails and delegate those best responded to by a staff member. Manage the rest.

BEYOND YOUR FIRST DAYS

Congratulations! You tackled the first days and weeks as a leader. You have a better understanding of your staff, what you want to accomplish, your financial outlook, who's who, and how you want to approach building strong relationships. You have met with the board of directors, and you know what they expect of you. Now it is time to concentrate on the most critical part of the job—fundraising. Fundraising will generate the necessary money and other resources to maintain operations and build a sustainable organization well into the future.

2

Fundraising Categories

THE MOST IMPORTANT ASPECT of your job as a leader is fundraising. This is where strategic thinking and strategic planning are vital to the operation and sustainability of the organization. As the leader, you will encounter obstacles that are not for the timid at heart. This is the area that takes stamina, courage, risk, desire, determination, and stubbornness. Yes, stubbornness helps. Fundraising is also the area that arouses high anxiety, agony, and fear. Don't be discouraged. To keep your doors open and provide good will, fundraising is a necessity, and you can become skillful at it.

Do you have a development director? If you are a small nonprofit, the leader will be responsible for the cultivation of major donors and fundraising activities. If you are mid-to-large nonprofit and you have a development director, stop right now, do cartwheels, and count your blessings. You just struck gold!

Your development director is responsible for planning, coordinating, and implementing long-term fundraising strategies. They will write the grants and send out proposals. They will research and cultivate new prospects, run special events and other fundraisers. They will also solicit major gifts, send direct marketing solicitations and appeals to individuals, and work closely with corporate sponsors and foundations. In other words, you will be the visionary and they will lead and manage fundraising and development activities. They will save you time, and you will oversee their activities and operations. You will meet with top supporters and VIPs. Isn't that grand?

Most nonprofits may be without a development director and all those responsibilities default to the executive-in-charge. Fundraising can arouse anxiety simply because it takes time, effort, high energy, and a positive attitude always.

The "time" factor caused me the greatest anxiety attacks. Most days, all my other responsibilities could easily have occupied my entire work day, but I had to juggle them while keeping my focus on fundraising because I understood that none of those other duties would matter much if we could not fund them. Fundraising shouts for constant attention. As a leader with a small staff, you may find fundraising daunting and overwhelming at times because the number one revenue driving mechanism for a nonprofit is fundraising. And yes, it takes time.

Donations for your organization will come from five primary groups: 1) individuals, board members, and volunteers; 2) corporations; 3) foundations; 4) special events; and 5) a rather amorphous category we will call other sources. Larger nonprofits may also have earned income, planned giving, and trusts, but the discussion here will focus on the categories just mentioned.

INDIVIDUALS, BOARD MEMBERS, AND VOLUNTEERS

As you enter the organization, you must identify who your top donors are and how to maintain an ongoing relationship with them. You probably have a donor database management system that contains the list of donors who have supported the organization over the years. If you don't have one, create one. There are plenty to choose from such as Raiser's Edge, eTapestry, DonorPerfect, Gift-Works, and The Databank. Do your research to find the best for your size organization. Donor database management systems save you time when organizing appeal letters.

Retaining individual donors requires several "touches" or "marketing communication" during the year through phone contacts, lunches or coffees, direct mail, e-newsletters, invitations to special events, or a combination of these. Typically, at least seven touches are the goal. Reach out and touch your supporters through various communication tools to keep them informed and engaged. Thank them often for their past contributions and respectfully ask for their continued support.

How do you better engage individuals? Invite them to be volunteers throughout the year for special events, office projects, other projects related to your organization, and/or committee membership. The more involved they are, the more committed to the mission they become. Then they give and tell others to give. Building individual relationships takes time, but it pays off in the long run.

Most organizations have a database filled with individuals. Learn the system to capitalize on those who have given regularly. Keep track of as much information as you can. Gather information on how much was given, when, and for what event or campaign. Identify individuals who are heavily invested in the organization. Are they volunteers? Are they board members? Should they be board members? How can you engage them?

Tips on Maintaining Individual Donors

✓ Do mass mailings at least two to four times a year. I eventually moved to quarterly mailings for a reason: communities are mobile. People move to new homes within the state or move out of state. The best method to ensure you have the most current address is to send mailings regularly. Also collect e-mails if possible to keep donors updated through e-newsletters.

✓ Update any mailings that are returned. If caught in time, there will be a forwarding address you can use to update the address in your donor database.

✓ Collect e-mails, preferably home e-mails, because business e-mails tend to change often.

✓ Whenever possible, collect phone numbers. This will allow a special touch, one you make by simply calling them to say thank you. Don't ask for money. Just say, "Thank you for supporting our organization," and tell what their support helps you with. This can be a good project for volunteers or board members.

Board members are individuals as well. Does everyone on the board give? I hope they do. That's a popular question that funders often ask when they do site visits. It is good to be able to tell them that one hundred percent of the board contributes to support the organization because they believe in the mission. It doesn't matter how much they give. In some instances, giving may involve purchasing a ticket to an event, buying auction items, or giving of their time, which is also of value. In the world of nonprofits that need money to run programs, giving money is extremely important.

If you have a board or board members who feel their time is valuable, just explain to them that funders ask specifically if board members invest their own money in the cause. Or be forthright and say to your board member, "Can I count on your $100 gift this year?" Hopefully, you know your board member and know his or her giving capacity. That may mean that instead of asking if you can count on their $100 gift, you ask if you can count on their $1000 gift.

Volunteers are an unbelievable force and resource when it comes to fundraising. Countless times, I have seen a volunteer who offered to help with an office project later donate towards the cause. Other volunteers work special events and end up being the main contributors purchasing silent auction items. Some just want to tell their friends and family about the organization through social media channels, which leads to new donors and increased awareness. You are wise to always welcome new volunteers who are dedicated to your organization and retain the seasoned ones. They can ultimately be the best investment for organizational growth.

CORPORATIONS

You should approach corporations for charitable giving. Many of them have a philanthropic arm or charitable giving program. Determine which strategies you want to use. Research the corporate market. One thing I did was research the corporate market while attending special events for other nonprofit organizations by looking at their sponsors list. I wrote down the sponsors' names to do an online search when I returned to my office—I found that some could possibly support the organization because the mission fell within their priority funding areas.

Another method I used was the *Book of Lists* produced by the *Denver Business Journal*. It was a gold resource when I was trying to outreach to businesses that might support my organization's cause. *The Book of Lists* features companies in their respective fields and industries and provides the names of the key decision makers, along with addresses and phone numbers. This type of resource creates endless opportunities to explore new territories or gain new corporate donors. Search your market to see if anyone is creating something like this in your area.

Newspapers and business magazine articles provide insight on a company's philanthropic direction. The articles prove to be a valuable resource for gauging whether a company's value system matches your organization. For instance, if you read the newspaper and find a company that has just awarded a school a million dollars, make a note of it and research what other causes they support. Of course, you could search the Internet until you glaze over or go blind, but I suggest that you invest the time by delving into the background, stories, and facts of potential supporters you find through media stories and reports.

FOUNDATIONS

Tackling foundations takes strategic planning. While I had some grant writing experience under my belt stemming from serving on various nonprofit boards, I never had training on grant writing proposals. When I was hired as the leader, I searched for and analyzed grants that had been previously written and submitted. To my surprise, there were no examples in the files. Instead, they were on the computer server. It took countless hours of review, but it was well worth the time. And after reviewing as many grants as my mind could handle without exploding, I better understood the structure, components, and dynamics of a grant. It probably took me a year before I could honestly say that I could write a successful grant warranting outstanding results.

If you have a development background or a development director on staff, you have nothing to worry about. Your development director will research, cultivate, and write grants. If you are an executive just entering the role of grant writing, I suggest that you take a grant writing course offered by nonprofits specializing in strengthening nonprofit leaders. Remember, grants are competitive. Gain the competitive edge by preparing strong grants that get attention.

Grant writing is an art. The most important parts of the grant include the cover letter and narrative. At the beginning of each year, prepare a cover letter that can be customized for each foundation. Customize the letter, using one paragraph to identify how your program best fits into the foundation's mission and priority funding areas. Develop the narrative and update it with current financial information that describes the success of your program. For instance, how many people did you serve in the program?

Tips on Gaining Respect from Foundations

✓ Always meet grant deadlines.

✓ Always complete any final report before reapplying.

✓ If they request additional information to be included in the grant, respond promptly.

✓ Foundation leaders may not have time to go to lunch with everyone they fund. Try to touch base with them at least once or twice a year through phone connections or e-mail.

✓ Touch base with them before submitting a grant. Let them know that you will be submitting a grant for their consideration.

✓ Always meet their yearly report deadlines. Without adhering to their report requirements, you could threaten future chances of receiving a grant.

✓ Don't be shy. Now is the time to be bold. You should request funds to provide services for your clients. Ask for what you need for your program. Review and analyze how much they give to other organizations. Try to be in the middle of the road if it is your first time applying. The objective is to start building.

GRANT WRITING GUIDELINES

Some foundations and corporations may give specific instructions and guidelines on writing grants. If they do not, one of the best formats I found was through the Colorado Common Grant site. I appreciate this format because it covers majority of the elements requested by many foundations and corporations. My suggestion would be to create a grant at the beginning of your fiscal year using the common grant categories. Below is a sample grant application outline. The advantage of using the common grant layout is that you will be prepared for almost any guidelines from foundations and corporations. After it is complete, you can cut and paste the pertinent elements into each grant for which you are applying. The main objective is to reduce the amount of time it takes to create a grant from scratch. Following the outline, you will find a few pointers on completing each section.

1. Cover Letter
   a) Does your mission match their priorities?
2. Narrative
   a) Background
   b) Goals and Objectives
   c) Inclusiveness/Diversity
   d) Board Involvement
   e) Evaluation

3. Attachments

    a) Current Financials

      (Balance Sheet and Profit & Loss)

    b) Fiscal Year-end (Balance Sheet and Profit & Loss)

    c) Audit (when applicable)

    d) Board of Directors Contact List

    e) 501(c)3 IRS Letter of Determination

    f) Nondiscrimination Policy

    g) Organizational Budget

    h) Program Budget

    i) Major Contributors

    j) Key Staff

    k) Evaluation

    l) Other

        Annual Report

        Testimonials

The Cover Letter

I discovered that the cover letter is your opportunity to define why you are requesting a grant. Study the funding priorities of the granting organization and consider those priorities when choosing which grants to apply for. Do not force your mission to fit their funding priorities because doing so is a waste of your time. In other words, if the granting organization supports K-12 arts and culture, your homeless program or dog rescue may not fit.

When preparing the cover letter, describe how the mission of your organization aligns with the grant making organization's funding priorities in one or two paragraphs. By doing so, you will give the grant director or committee a chance to understand why they should continue reading before they get to the narrative.

Narrative

Now shine—paint a clear and concise picture of your organization. If this is the first time pursuing a grant from a specific foundation, now is the time to make your organization known to them. Make it stand out. Make it memorable. Let your organization shine with vibrant, vivid color to demonstrate why your organization should be considered for a grant. Remember, competition is steep. Don't let that stop you. Keep your mission at the forefront of your mind. Your nonprofit has people to serve. Never forget that!

If your organization has applied to the grant maker in previous years, you may add current program statistics to show progression.

In the narrative, describe how the organization was founded, why, and by whom? What community need were the founders trying to address? How long has the organization been around? What are your accomplishments? Who is your target population? How have you made a difference? If your organization is new and you don't have a track record, describe your goals, what you anticipate providing, and when you will provide it.

Outline up to three goals your organization is working on for the current year. In some instances, your goals may be ongoing. For instance, a primary goal may be to eliminate homelessness. Identify current goals towards those efforts.

The reason you exist is to drive programs that help the citizens in your community, state, and/or region. Tell them who you serve; identify the population. This will be easier if you collect demographic data yearly on the number served, ages served, ethnicity, counties served, and economic levels. Get specific with what you track. Include things like age, gender, race, creed, religion, marital status, income level, and whether they are insured, underinsured, or uninsured. Compile this into a report you can pull from in preparing grants. If you are applying for a program grant, this data will help you explain how the grant funds will be used in the program. Specific demographics on the people you serve can prove useful when foundations request such information be provided with your grant proposal.

In today's world, it is imperative that your organization work towards inclusivity. Who have you recruited to volunteer for your organization and be on your staff and board that demonstrate your values in being inclusive of age, ethnicity, gender orientation, and disability? Make sure a statement about this is included in your grant.

Describe the board of director's roles and responsibilities. If they are developing a strategic plan, you don't have to go into detail. Let the grant makers know about governance roles and how the board contributes to the organization.

Of course, the nonprofit lifeblood is known as volunteers, so be sure to talk about them, too. Without them, many nonprofits would crumble or close their doors. Volunteers save the organization thousands of dollars annually through their work. Let your grant makers know how they contribute to your organization, what they do, and how many hours they work.

Program evaluation differs for each organization. You may offer surveys to each of your program participants, which is a great idea, providing you get surveys back. Survey Monkey is free and it is one of my favorite online tools. More people are willing to take a survey if it is a short format, so keep it short. Take every opportunity you get to collect evaluations of your program. The grant makers are searching for impact. How do you measure results? How impactful is your program?

Attachments

By preparing attachments at the beginning of the year, you save time when applying for grants. Certain attachments can be prepared in advance, such as the fiscal year-end, audit, board of director's contact list, 501(c)3 IRS Letter of Determination, Nondiscrimination Policy, organizational budget, program budget, major contributors, and key staff descriptions.

Except for current financials, store attachments in a file or computer folder for easy access. When applying for a grant, the grantors will request the most recent current financials.

Some grant-makers may request other types of attachments including annual reports and testimonials; those fantastic, glossy annual reports that some nonprofits are lucky enough to have. If you do not have an annual report, create one. The report will show how your organization advances and impacts the community. It helps your organization stand out. On occasion, you may also want to add testimonials you have collected from program recipients to demonstrate how your program impacts their lives.

Restricted and Unrestricted Grants

Restricted grants must be used for a specific purpose outlined in the grant donor's agreement. For instance, if you applied for a grant for programs and you receive the award because the foundation wants to support programs *only*, then create a tracking code or accounting code for the money received. If you track receipts and expenditures, you can print out a report showing when the grant funds were received and how they were distributed at the end of the grant cycle. Accountability to the granting foundation or donor is paramount.

Unrestricted grants can be used to maintain operational expenses such as utilities, equipment, rent, salaries, etc. You can use unrestricted grants for programs as well, as long as you have general operations covered throughout the year.

Tips on Grant Writing

✓ Before you get started on writing grants, review previous grants received. Read any comments or feedback received from foundations or donors. The feedback allows you to correct any misconstrued information from previous grants.

✓ Make a note to include all necessary components and avoid unnecessary documentation. For example, if the comment is "lacks statistical data," collect the statistical data you have available and research how to locate more. Grant makers requesting more statistical data are often referring to the number of people served in your program.

✓ If you do not have a grant writer or development manager, you should set aside one day a week to concentrate on writing grants. If feasible, stay home and write to eliminate or reduce interruptions from staff, phones, and other projects pertaining to business operations.

✓ If you have time constraints related to writing grants, hire a contractual grant writer, providing your budget allows it. If you are going to write the grants yourself, know that grants take differing amounts of time to write. Some grants take an hour to write, others two hours, and larger grants take four to eight hours. Plan your time wisely. If you have too many grants, not enough time, and cannot hire a grant writer, recruit someone from the board of directors or a volunteer to help you.

✓ To meet grant submission deadline requirements, create a yearly grant deadline calendar. Thankfully, not all grant proposals have deadlines, but when they do, stick to them to avoid elimination. Grant administrators have rules to follow.

No matter how fabulous the grant, if it comes in after dead-line, you will not be considered. Don't let that happen to you. Pay close attention to deadlines.

✓ Break your grant writing into seasons: January—June or July--December. Arrange the season when you have fewer special event fundraising activities. During the grant writing season, review all the grants you need to complete the entire year. Write your grants and place them in a tickler file. Then review, revise, and update them as needed a month before the due date. Send them to the foundation one week prior to deadline. Yes, one week before the deadline. Why? Because sometimes the funder places a courtesy call and says, "Oh by the way, you left out this. Please send it to us by deadline."

✓ If you have special events throughout the year, be sure to schedule your grant writing days in between special events. This takes advance planning on your end, but it helps reduce stress.

✓ Write clear and concise sentences. Build a good case for support. Don't overkill. Be accurate and truthful. Don't embellish so much that it sounds like a fairy tale.

✓ Stay within the guidelines when it comes to type of font, pitch, number of pages allowed, number of copies to include with the packet, and where to mail or e-mail the packet.

✓ Review, review, review! That's the best advice I can give you. Have your grant outline in front of you. Did you include all the attachments they need? Good. Now double check.

Fund Searching Strategies

If your organization is new, you are probably searching for grant funds from foundations, corporations, and government entities.

Funding research is vital for startups and equally vital for the growth potential of established nonprofits. Your local library is an excellent starting place. There are literally thousands of charitable foundations. Instead of spending several hours typing search words, head to the library one afternoon. It will save you time, because in the reference section at the public library you will find a foundation directory containing the information on foundations, corporations, and government entities that grant funds. You will find their addresses, contact information, websites, phone numbers, their primary funding areas, and other relevant data to help you identify grants that specifically fit your organization. You can also subscribe to the Foundation Directory online for a broad list of grant makers.

When you find a promising foundation, read through their mission, priority funding areas, and the average amount they grant. The information provided includes contact information, phone numbers, budget size, restrictions, and a brief history. Look for the type of organizations they supported the previous year to gauge if your organization is similar. How much did they award? This is critical information to determine how much to ask for when writing your grant.

If after reviewing the foundation's profile you have concluded that your mission fits well with their priority, move to the next phase. Write down their website and contact information. Review their website, read through the guidelines, and make note of the deadline date. Add the deadline date to your grant calendar.

I know you're excited. You have found a foundation that could support your organization with $10,000 or more. But wait. You now need to make a courtesy call to the foundation's public affairs officer or grants officer to determine if your organization is truly a good fit. Do you need to be invited to apply or is it open to any organization within their guidelines? Why the phone call? They don't know you, and you must create a bridge of introduction to become known.

Keep in mind that you have competition, and you can find them on the funding organization's website. Is your organization better than the competition? Is it comparable? Is your program better? You may need to do some research and probing to get the answers to these questions. But there is good news. Many foundations fund organizations for two consecutive years, then skip a year. You can use that to your advantage by applying on the year that a competing organization cannot apply. Go for it! Apply.

SPECIAL EVENTS

Small nonprofits needing revenue—especially during the inevitable funding valleys that nonprofits experience during the year—may consider special events. It takes time, effort, energy, and a staff or a group of dedicated volunteers to produce a successful event, but the rewards can be grand. Special events can increase awareness of your organization and programs, leading to heightened media coverage, that can help you gain new corporate sponsors, and can increase donations and volunteers. The real income may come from a silent or live auction if you include one as part of the event.

Before you begin planning a special event, know that there are also disadvantages. Special events are time consuming, which may be especially problematic if you have a small staff. You may break even after working countless hours and losing precious sleep. So, what are some of the best ways to approach special events?

1. If you have a small staff, only plan one or two major special events per year. Plan one during the first quarter and one during the third quarter. Spread them out.
2. Bring in community organizers. Third- party organizers are king! They plan, organize, coordinate, and implement all

the aspects of the special event and ask very little of you and your staff. As the executive, you will oversee any budgetary consequences to holding the event. For instance, the organizer may want to be paid a small stipend or salary. You will determine how much time they spend and decide on a fair payment scale that does not eat away at the proceeds raised. If they plan on raising $30,000 for the organization, then it's fair to pay 10% or more back to the event organizer. They saved you time and money.

3. Another way to relieve staff of the time commitment involved with special events is to recruit volunteers to take on some of the responsibilities. Let's say you want to do a happy hour. Ask your volunteers to secure a location for it. You would attend the event to speak or recruit a board member or advisory member to speak on behalf of the organization.

4. Consider having a house party. House parties are a great way to introduce potential supporters to the organization and draw continuing supporters. The mix and mingle of these two groups might prove beneficial to the organization. A short program at the event is helpful, and provides an opportunity for people to donate. That may be as simple as donation envelopes available at the venue or a few moments during the program devoted to a donation plea.

5. Consider including a silent and/or live auction at the event. Typically, auctions are tied to a grand event like a dinner or gala. Remember that auctions are work. Auction item donations must be solicited and collected. The auction display must be set up and taken down at the end of the event. Someone will have to coordinate the collection of money and distribution of items to successful bidders. A team of dedicated and committed volunteers are needed to pull off a successful auction fundraiser.

6. If you know of top talent scheduling concerts in your area, consider approaching them to see if they might be willing to donate a portion of ticket sales to your organization at one of their concerts.

OTHER SOURCES OF INCOME

Besides the normal channel of obtaining revenue through individuals, corporations, foundations, and special events, you may want to consider other sources, such as earned income, planned giving, and endowments.

EARNED INCOME

When the economy takes a downward slope affecting revenue, do what the Girl Scouts do: start selling! No, not delicious cookies, sell goods and services that may bring revenue into the organization. Is it something you can package and sell? Do you have knowledge to share with others? Can you create training sessions or seminars and charge a fee?

Of course, whatever you decide, do some market research to determine what your competitors are doing and avoid duplicating anything another nonprofit is already doing. Think about collaborative efforts and partnerships with companies and service providers. Also avoid any legal repercussions with for-profit companies who may think you're infringing on their territory. When competing with for-profit entities, consider market share. How well can you compete? How is the for-profit entity going to react?

Every nonprofit aims for sustainability in today's business climate. Finding innovative avenues for making earned income will help ensure that you can remain viable as a nonprofit.

PLANNED GIVING

Planned giving is a novel idea and a win-win for all involved. Tracking down lifelong philanthropists can be a challenge, but individuals owning real estate, stocks, valuable artwork or artifacts may elect to donate them to a charitable organization. Your organization may become the recipient of funds of a life insurance policy or be a will beneficiary. Your organization could be included in a workplace giving program. An individual could add charitable contributions funneled through an individual retirement account. These are sources you may not have thought of until you begin to dig into potential planned giving sources.

ENDOWMENT

An endowment is a gift or bequest made through an investment in which funds are invested, the principal remains intact, and the funds distributed come from the earnings from the investment. That means that endowments may come through money earned from stocks, bonds, mutual funds, and other investments. Because the donation is tied to investments, it will fluctuate over time, depending on the markets invested in. Most of your endowment funds may come from individuals wanting to invest in the organization. Nonprofits can start an endowment fund and build on it each year. The higher the amount, the more interest dividends are available to support and sustain the programs of the organization.

●　●　●　●　●　●

The ability to raise funds is critical to the survival and success of any nonprofit. As the leader, your commitment, determination, and tenacious fundraising efforts moves the organization forward. It is easy to become too enmeshed in the day-to-day activities of leading and managing a nonprofit. Sometimes fundraising stays on the list of things not yet attended to for long periods of time because you may not see it as one of the critical problems to be solved immediately. Effective fundraising is one of the most significant responsibilities you have as leader, and the development of tactics to meet your fundraising plan requires ongoing attention and effort.

Overall, fundraising is critical in maintaining the programs and providing vital services to those in need. As the organization starts to maintain a steady flow of funds, you must strive to preserve and increase that level of funding. Should funding levels drop, you must consider other sources of income, such as the earned income, planned giving, and endowments.

Fundraising evolves through your consistent and productive efforts. Without sufficient funds, the organization will be unable to achieve its mission of bringing positive transformation to peoples' lives. With sufficient funds, not only will you be able to fulfill your mission, the organization may be able to touch more lives in more profound ways than you could have imagined. And that makes it all worthwhile.

3

Engaging the Board of Directors

A S THE LEADER OF a nonprofit, the most important relationship you have is the relationship with your board. That relationship began when they hired you and will continue as they evaluate you, advise you, and monitor your organization's programs.

Nonprofit boards have many responsibilities that can be broken down into three fundamental categories: fiduciary, decision making, and compliance. Your organization's board is not only responsible for ensuring that there are adequate funds to run the organization, but also for ensuring that those funds and the organization's other assets are given proper oversight. They also make decisions and monitor operations, programs, and services to ensure that they are in keeping with good practices, are effective, and are consistent with the nonprofit's mission and purpose. And they ensure that the nonprofit is in compliance with laws and regulations applying to it.

Beyond these basic responsibilities, the board has responsibility for maintaining and enhancing the nonprofit's public standing and public image. And collectively, they are not only your boss they can be your front-line advisor.

INTERACTING WITH THE BOARD OF DIRECTORS

As the leader, you report to the board of directors or trustees on a regular basis. I called on the board for advice, suggestions, and recommendations as needed, especially when I was working on strategic direction that could affect the organization's finances.

Through the years, I learned that it is best to keep the board advised on the organization's financial and operational matters on an ongoing basis. For instance, I informed the board when there were changes in funding and personnel, when office infrastructure needed revamping, and when program elements no longer were working. I even gave the board office lease expiration dates.

You should build a trusting relationship with your board by touching base with them once or twice a month. Take time to schedule a monthly meeting with the board president or executive committee to discuss financial concerns, infrastructure problems, or program changes before the monthly board meeting. This gives you the opportunity to share concerns and identify solutions to problems.

Your board is there to ensure that you are meeting their expectations and the financial obligations of the organization. They are there to act as advisors and approve annual budgets. It is good practice to have the treasurer review and approve draft audits before they are finalized. This will help you ensure that the board understands the audit and how it creates direction for the next year and beyond.

The board will require you to prepare the monthly financials to include profit and loss (P&L), balance sheet, cash flow statements, and a monthly budget or financial recap. The financials are critical pieces of information that aid them in making sound governance and fiduciary decisions. This is the nitty-gritty part of the job. As the leader, it is important for you to review all the financials and double-check to make sure your bookkeeper or accountant has placed the received funds in the appropriate category. By reviewing the financials before the board meetings, you can prepare financial notes to share with the board about any activity that has taken place.

Tips on Board Governance/Involvement/Interaction

✓ Prepare a monthly executive staff report for the board to keep them informed of the activities that took place with fundraising, operations, programs, and upcoming events.

✓ Ask employees to participate in the executive staff report by listing the projects they have completed as well as upcoming projects with which board members can become involved.

✓ Don't isolate the board of directors. Remember, they want you to succeed for the betterment of the organization.

✓ Never talk badly about a board member to another board member or to other community leaders. It is important to stay in the neutral zone—or as I like to call it, the "diplomatic zone."

✓ Do not argue with board members. Explain your position and reasoning, but don't be argumentative.

RECRUITING BOARD MEMBERS

Board members are term limited, except for startup organizations where a board member may stay on longer until the organization is stable. You will be involved in identifying and recruiting board members due to normal attrition. I found that the best way to identify and recruit board members is through the cultivation of relationships with funders and volunteers. Could one or more be possible board members? If they are heavily involved, it may be time to meet with them one-on-one and see if they would be interested in serving on the board.

How about the networking groups you belong to? Who in them has strong skills in finance, law, marketing, public relations, social media, IT, human resources, or other talents important to your organization? When it comes to identifying potential board members, think about the skill sets missing. Create a matrix of your current board members, determine who is rotating off the board, and add to your matrix the skills and talents you need. This will help in identifying who is missing from the board.

When selecting board members, consider diversity in every area: race, age, gender, professional background, geography, etc. I suggest you aim for diversity in many areas.

BOARD MEETINGS

How often should you meet with the board? As often as they want. But seriously, I recommend meeting with the board once a month, providing you have something concrete and substantial to share with them about the financial outlook of the organization or you are requesting their assistance on a special assignment.

What about calling for an emergency meeting? If your organization has experienced a huge drop in funding that threatens your operations and programs, it is best to call an emergency meeting. Contact your board president/chair right away. He or she will connect with the rest of the board. Your role is to help solve the problem. While they are working on scheduling the meeting, you can begin to develop a strategy on recovering lost revenue. Think about how you would create new revenue streams.

BOARD GIFT GIVING AND FUNDRAISING INVOLVEMENT

Should board members give an annual gift? This is a question often asked. Some board members feel they do not have to give a monetary gift because they serve and give of their time; others think it is a necessity. I am in the camp that believes board members should give an annual gift. Why? Because it suggests full buy-in from them. Can you expect anyone else to fund your organization if the board does not demonstrate its buy-in by donating?

Let's look at this in another way. Suppose you are a business owner investing thousands of your own money to build your business. One day you decide that you need other investors to grow your business. They will see your passion through your own investment. The same holds true for nonprofits. If board members invest in the organization through their monetary gifts, foundations and corporations being asked to give are more likely to donate. You will find that it adds credibility to your grant requests when you can say that one hundred percent of the board participates through their monetary gifts. It lets the potential funder know that the board is fully committed to the mission and goals of the organization; and you will find that their dedication carries a lot of weight.

What about fundraising activities? Should your board be involved? This is a fun-duh-mental question, and the answer is yes.

Fundraising takes many forms. If you hold special events, you might have the board involved by manning the information booth or helping with registration to meet and greet attendees. If you hold a gala, consider having some of the board members serve on the gala committee or ask one to chair the committee. Ask them to take a development workshop through a nonprofit educational center to increase their ability to help with development. The board should also consider creating their own fundraising events to support the organization.

Ultimately, there are many ways a board member can help raise funds. Ask for their help and involvement. It will be good for the organization, good for your relationship with the board, and good for the goal of board engagement.

BOARD EVALUATION OF LEADER PERFORMANCE

Because you were hired by the board and report to them, you will be evaluated by them. This is an opportunity for them to assess how you performed against their expected outcomes. What they are looking for is how much money was raised, whether you met or exceeded budget projections, and how well you handled staff and operations.

There are a couple of ways the evaluation can take place. Everyone on the board may be asked to write up their analysis of your performance as a leader. Alternatively, the president or executive committee may perform the evaluation.

The evaluation should be done on an annual basis, but sometimes schedules become too busy, causing a delay. As the leader, you are entitled to ask for a performance evaluation on or near your anniversary hire date or at the end of each fiscal year. Just as the board wants to assess how you have done, you want to know where you stand, if you are doing a good job, and in what areas, if any, you need to improve. This is a great time to see if you are on the right track.

When it comes to evaluations, always remember that you are the organization's steward. And the reason you are there is to serve the community. No matter what the mission, you are there to serve the community. So, listen closely to the board's comments and avoid becoming defensive. Take the constructive criticism and channel it towards improving the organization's operations.

I admit that I have heard from some executive leaders who felt their evaluations were brutal and who were offended by the comments they received. You are there to work with the board of directors in service to the community, and they must ensure that you are following the doctrine as outlined for the organization to be successful.

However, if you determine there is a lack of support from the board of directors, consult with an external leader confidentially and devise a clear strategy on working with the board.

● ● ● ● ● ●

Boards exist to provide the necessary oversight and governance to nonprofits. As a leader, your ability to effectively interact with your board is critical to the smooth functioning of your organization. When you nurture a trusting relationship between you and your board, not only will you improve your chances of gaining their support for your decisions, but you will also have their valuable counsel when you want and need it. Avoid unnecessary conflict with your board, find peaceful solutions when conflict is unavoidable, and remember that both you and the board share the common goal of doing what is best for the organization and those it serves. When you can hold that truth, the organization's mission has a chance to thrive.

4

The Financial Review

ONE OF THE MOST critical and significant roles of leadership is financial oversight. The leader gauges the sustainability of the organization by analyzing financials monthly. There are several financial reports to review.

- ✓ Balance Sheet or Statement of Financial Position
- ✓ Income Statement or Profit and Loss (P&L) Statement
- ✓ Profit and Loss Year to Date (YTD)
- ✓ Cash Flow
- ✓ Budget
- ✓ Audit
- ✓ Reserves

When I first started, I printed the P&L and balance sheet for the previous year. My objective was to paint a financial picture to determine the peaks and valleys of the overall financial outlook.

By analyzing the financials, I understood how much was spent on monthly operations (rent, utilities, and salaries) and how much was spent on programs. I could determine the time of year grants were received and examine when funding arrived from direct mail campaigns, special events, individual contributions, and corporate support.

As leader, I had to maintain those funding sources, plus apply strategies on how to increase funding sources during a period. By studying the finances, I could back into the figures. For instance, if I found a grant was received in March, I would pull the grant report to see when the grant was submitted. Then I could determine how long it would take to receive the funds after submitting the grant proposal and being awarded a grant.

When you are reviewing each of these reports, look for any areas that need improvement. Of course, you will concentrate on the bottom line. How do your overall assets compare to last year? Are they increasing or decreasing? How much and how fast? Is it enough to keep the program(s) going? What else do you need to do to increase your financial position?

BALANCE SHEET/STATEMENT OF FINANCIAL POSITION

When reviewing the balance sheet, you should analyze the assets, liabilities, and organizational equity. The balance sheet provides checking account and investment account balances, and you should monitor these accounts regularly. In addition, review the liabilities, accounts payable, and payroll obligations. The balance sheet's equity section indicates the net worth of the organization, which helps you assess the organization's viability. By studying the balance sheet monthly, you will have an overall sense of the organization's financial health, which will help you make informed decisions to positively impact its financial future and strategic direction.

INCOME STATEMENT/P&L

When analyzing the P&L statement, examine each line item to gauge where the money is coming from. Do you need more donations from individuals? How about corporations? Are they engaged in your organization? If not, what program or event can you get them involved with? Did you continue to receive support from all the foundations you sought grants from? Did they give the same amount as the previous year? More? Less? If some foundations funded you in previous years but not the current year, why? How do you plan on reaching out to them again? Through—a major fundraiser, campaign, or what?

Also, examine your organization's expenses. Are you staying within budget? Are there any expenses you can cut, such as phone, rental expenses, office supplies, or equipment leasing? If you are leasing the office space, when does the lease expire?

The leader must uphold the highest of values in honesty and integrity, particularly in this area. The accountability of all money received and dispersed relies on general accounting practices and systems. Subsequently, the board treasurer and all board members, hold fiduciary responsibilities to ensure accounting systems are in place and no fraudulent activities are taking place.

PROFIT AND LOSS YEAR-TO-DATE

Compare your expenses to last year's expenses. Are they similar? Are you overspending in certain areas? If so, why? If your expenses are higher, what is driving that? Take control of your organization's spending by paying close attention to staff spending habits to ensure that there is always enough money for the mission.

Also compare the amount of funds raised from individuals, special events, corporations, grants, and other income sources. You will want to review expenses related to payroll, workers compensation, insurance, programs, equipment, rent, office supplies, and marketing. Look for expenses that seem excessive, research their causes when you find them, and act if needed to reduce future expenses in these areas.

BUDGET

Examine the budget to analyze expected monetary needs. Plan to increase revenues by a certain percentage and conceptualize best methods to do that, but be realistic. Do you plan on serving more people next year? How do you intend to cover additional expenses? Do you need more staff? How will you pay for more staff? Your budget is your guide and your roadmap for creating a successful year. It is up to you to raise funds to cover the cyclical expenses associated with running a nonprofit.

CASH FLOW STATEMENT

Cash flow statements will show the operating activities and net income position of the organization. Observe and monitor the investments, such as certificates of deposit, endowments and reserves.

Grow these accounts for sustainability. Do be aware, however, that your cash position may fluctuate if your investments are tied to the volatile stock market. Monitor cash flow statements regularly since investment and financial position fluctuates month to month. Your cash flow may be negative on some months and positive on others. Don't be alarmed with the negatives unless it is at the end of your fiscal period which may indicate a deficit in funds. For example, let's say you have a negative cash flow in January but a positive one in February after receiving a large grant. Since cash flow fluctuation is typical, monitoring it monthly will help you determine if you are generating sufficient cash for business operations.

AUDITS

An audit is great on two accounts: it provides accurate data on operations and it is a great planning tool for devising an annual budget. Review the statement of financial position. Understand contributions that are restricted or unrestricted. You can refer to the financial notes found at the back of the audit to determine why the funds are restricted or unrestricted. Place emphasis on contributions from individuals, corporations, foundations, and special events to help you calculate the funding percentage from each group. By understanding the percentages, you can better comprehend how well your fundraising efforts are working and better assess what changes need to be made to your fundraising goals and their execution.

For example, if the audits show that 8% of funds have come from individuals, 12% from corporations, 50% from foundations, and 30% from special events, you might want to review that year's fundraising plans for garnering individual contributions to determine how to increase the percentage from 8% to 9% or more. This might require additional mailings or personal phone calls to more individuals to ask for donations. You can then assess each other funding source in a similar way and determine what changes need to be made to increase revenues for each of them.

Notice the expenses relating to the implementation of program services and special events. Your objective is to keep expenses for programs and special events within budget.

By analyzing the latest audit, you can evaluate how well the organization performed. The audit should be completed by an external or independent auditor who verifies that appropriate financial internal controls exist within the organizational structure.

RESERVES

To a certain degree, reserves are like endowments. Whenever your organization raises funds beyond expectations for the fiscal year, place some funds in reserve. For instance, let's say that by the end of the fiscal year, your organization has received $50,000 more than budgeted. Place a portion, maybe 30-50%, of those funds in reserve. The remaining funds could be carried forward and used for programs. It is possible that you may need to use those reserves if the organization experiences a short-fall down the road.

●　　●　　●　　●　　●　　●

Ultimately, it is the responsibility of the leader to ensure sufficient funds are available to maintain operations and to pay program expenses. The leader must retain a strong financial position. By analyzing all the financial statements and making decisions based on your evaluation, you can control the income and expenses of the entire organization and position it for future growth.

5

Compliance

IF YOU ARE A small nonprofit, you probably don't have a legal department, but nonprofits have legal obligations that must be met annually to stay in compliance with state and federal laws. The best resource is the Secretary of State website for your state. Keep in mind that while federal laws are the same for every state, state laws differ from state to state. Start with your local Secretary of State to learn what laws pertain to your organization.

Staying in compliance can relate to many things including registration, license, insurance, lease agreements, employment contracts, employment manuals, federal posters, employee policies, sales tax, labor laws, and IRS rules and regulations. Become familiar with those areas that apply to your organization through IRS website, workshops, and research at the library or online.

SECRETARY OF STATE

At the end of each fiscal year, a nonprofit is required to file a renewal. For instance, in Colorado, you must renew before the fifteenth day of the fifth month if the charitable organization has solicited contributions. If your organization qualifies (check with the Secretary of State on requirements), to file you must first have an auditor prepare an audit and a 990. The figures found on the 990 are used to file the renewal. The cost of the renewal is minimal. As a matter of fact, the fines are higher than the renewal amount.

I recommend that you start preparing for the audit the first quarter of the year. Keep in mind that you may have to file an extension to avoid fines. If you forget, you will receive a late fee notice. Check with your local Secretary of State's website on fee structure, including late fines.

The Secretary of State offers business services you will need to stay in compliance. You will use them to file periodic reports, change an address, change your organization's name, obtain a certificate of good standing, and search for information.

DEPARTMENT OF TREASURY

The Department of Treasury is an important part of the compliance process. This is where you file the quarterly unemployment insurance. If you use QuickBooks, for instance, an unemployment report is generated each quarter. Fill in the employment amounts, make payments, and then send to Department of Treasury.

INTERNAL REVENUE SERVICE

What about 941s? Okay, here's a story for you. One day as I was driving into work, I received a phone call from one of my staff members. She was petrified. There standing before her in the office were two IRS agents. I could hear her heart pounding through the phone. She whispered into the receiver, "What should I do?"

"Ask them what they want," I whispered back in my most calm and collected tone.

She asked them what they wanted. "They want the past due 941s," she reported.

I told her that this was not a problem, I would be in the office shortly and we would track down the missing 941s.

It turned out that during the six-month transitional period between executive directors, no 941 federal tax returns were sent to the IRS. The IRS representatives were stopping by as a courtesy because they thought it was unusual. After I explained the transition, they requested that I send in the 941s by the end of the month.

This was a good lesson, and it led me to create a 941 calendar. I never ran into that situation again. Thankfully, all the 941s were paid in full and still in QuickBooks for easy printout. All I had to do was send them to my IRS agents.

Hopefully, this story will inspire you to check your own organization's 941 compliance. If you are a new nonprofit leader, don't panic. Create a calendar. The 941s are due quarterly. Complete the form indicating the organization's Employee Identification Number (EIN#), how many employees you have, employee wages, federal income withheld, taxable wages and tips, any adjustments, and tax liability for three months. Do this quarterly and send in your payment voucher along with your 941.

It's not a scary form. If you are using QuickBooks as your accounting software, most of the information will come from that. QuickBooks will generate the 941. Simply complete it, print it, and send it to the IRS.

But what if I discovered that my organization had not paid its federal income taxes that day the IRS paid a visit? There may have been late fees. To avoid penalties, process the 941 and payments quarterly.

941

Stay in compliance with IRS rules and regulations. If you have paid employees and staff wages, you will need to file a 941 each quarter with the IRS office in your region. The 941 identifies wages paid, federal income tax withheld, social security, Medicare taxes, and any adjustments to sick pay, tips, or insurance. You must file quarterly after you have submitted the first 941, even if you have no wages to report each quarter.

IRS agents may pay you a friendly, unexpected visit if you neglect to file your 941 as required. Agents may show up unannounced if you neglect to file for a period after having a track record of filing on a regular basis. They will ask a series of questions to better understand why you haven't filed and check to see if there are any unpaid taxes and/or penalties that may apply. Add to your calendar schedule April, July, October, and January. Those are the months you will need to file the 941.

If you change your name or address, don't forget to notify the IRS.

To complete the 941, you will need to have several pieces of information:

1. Employer Identification Number (EIN), the nine-digit number you will find on your Letter of Determination
2. Wages, tips, other compensation
3. Income tax withheld
4. Adjustments of withheld income tax (if applicable)
5. Taxable Social Security
6. Taxable Medicare wages
7. Sick pay adjustments (if applicable)
8. Overpayment (about which you probably received a notice from the IRS to include on the 941).

Submit the form. Make an electronic copy for your files in case the original is not received by the IRS because it has been lost in the mail or inadvertently sent to the wrong region. It is better to have a copy than to try to recreate the 941.

If you have paid staff, the 941 is the Employer's Quarterly Federal Tax Return that presents the amount of income tax, social security tax, etc., withheld from staff paychecks, along with the organization's portion of staff taxes.

990

As a charitable nonexempt 501(c)3 organization, you should file a 990 if you are securing $200,000 or more in revenues or $500,000 or more in assets. It is a comprehensive form detailing the financial position of the organization. Depending on the size of the organization, you may complete a 990EZ, 990, or 990-T. Admittedly, as the leader, you will want to recruit someone with a CPA background to help you complete the forms or hire a CPA firm to do them. Prepare for the numerous questions asked on the form that the CPA may not know. To prepare for the 990, here is a list of items you will need:

1. Most current audit (because a large portion of the information transfers from the audit to the 990)
2. The names and titles of officers, directors, trustees, key employees, and highest compensated employees
3. Independent contractors with $100,000 or more in compensation
4. The names, addresses, and amount contributed by major contributors
5. The answers to board governance questions, such as: Do you have a whistleblower policy? Do you have a record retention policy? Do you have a conflict of interest policy?

After the 990 is complete, ensure that the board treasurer and president/chair of the board review it. Once the 990 has received approval, file it. Go to the state's secretary of state website to complete the registration process. They will request information found on the 990. Place a copy of the 990 on required sites for public disclosure.

As for the 990-tax exempt form, which is filed annually, this document shows that your nonprofit organization is exempt from federal income taxes. Filing the 990 depends on the tax exemption status. For additional information, visit https:/www.irs.gov/.

OTHER IMPORTANT DOCUMENTS

Established organizations keep copies of the Articles of Incorporation and Bylaws as part of permanent recordkeeping. Also maintain an IRS Letter of Determination on file that states the organization's tax-exempt status.

6

People Make the Difference

IT IS NO SECRET that people who devote time to nonprofit organizations are there because they want to make a difference in other people's lives. These caring individuals aspire to assist people who are experiencing hardship, suffering from illness, struggling financially, or are disadvantaged. They believe in helping people who are sick and shut-in, homeless, or disabled. The people working in nonprofits are caring individuals who unselfishly devote their time and energy to serve others and lend a helping hand. No wonder individuals channeling their energy towards a good cause feel empowered and emotionally connected. Some work for free (as volunteers), while others require compensation.

Small nonprofits have a challenge when it comes to hiring staff because they have limited monetary resources. What if you cannot compensate staff? What if you don't have enough staff to perform all the necessary duties of the organization? What will you do? There are commonalities among all businesses, whether for profit or non-profit—management, bookkeeping or accounting, marketing, communication, IT and web development usually among them. People such as you, as the leader, make a difference in the day-to-day operations and in the lives of those being served. Organizations cannot operate without people performing those functions.

Many nonprofits are woefully understaffed. There might be a couple of staff members, a few staff members, or just you. If you are well-funded, hire staff. Then you can delegate and distribute the workload to ensure that all duties are covered.

During my tenure as executive director, I started with two part-time staff members, a part-time program manager and a part-time communication director. All other duties fell on my shoulders. How do you serve hundreds of program recipients with very little staff? I will share with you how to stretch your budget.

My organization's recipient waiting list seemed a mile long with breast cancer patients desperately needing their monthly bills to be paid through our services. Of course, I wanted to serve as many people as financially possible. I had a multitude of responsibilities, and my work was cut out for me. I needed staff. If you are in a similar position and the budget allows, some might be hired and others brought in on a contractual basis. Some might be unpaid interns, while others might be volunteers. Remember, nonprofits have one strong advantage over for-profit businesses: nonprofits can recruit volunteers to perform the work, saving the organization thousands of dollars annually. If you want to grow a nonprofit, I have found that you need to recruit reliable and dependable volunteers.

Remarkably, I recruited over forty-five trusted volunteers to perform fundraising assignments and I trained numerous interns to complete office tasks. I also contracted a few people to provide specialized services such as bookkeeping, grant writing, and technology.

My advice to you is to hire, train, recruit, or contract people who are dedicated to the cause and can help the organization flourish.

Whether an organization has one person or hundreds of people, there is much work to be done. There are nine critical areas to cover within an organization: leadership, development, bookkeeping, grant writing, programs, communications, fundraising (special events), administration, and IT.

Below, I highlight positions suitable for small nonprofits that cover these nine areas. Keep in mind that the people you hire should have the appropriate education, credentials, knowledge, and skills to perform the job. In addition, it is not necessary to hire for every position I list below. You determine what pertains to your organization and budget. I want to stress that nonprofits operate like any other business in that there is an abundance of work to be done, and the leader must find the right people to complete the work.

First, we will look at the positions and duties needed to operate a small organization. These positions coincide with the nine critical areas relevant to operations. Second, we will examine the best characteristics to consider when searching for a person to fill each of these positions. And, finally, we will discuss how to compensate staff on a minimal budget.

THE LEADER

As mentioned earlier, the leader's responsibilities are mammoth. In a nutshell, the leader is responsible for providing management, direction, and vision. He or she oversees operations, programs, staff, and volunteers. The leader develops long-range strategies to achieve the organization's mission and accomplishes annual goals and objectives, with the support of the board of directors. Fundraising activities and increasing revenues are paramount, and they constitute a major responsibility of the leader. The organization's leader is charged with cultivating and building relationships, along with building collaborations and partnerships. Hiring staff, managing finances, and developing budgets are equally important. Particularly in small and/or new organizations, it is the leader who writes grants, develops employment policies, manages legal issues and develops programs.

Because there is depth and breadth to the leader's responsibilities, they should be skilled in entrepreneurship, organizational management, and problem solving. Furthermore, they should be knowledgeable about marketing, public relations, and public speaking.

What kinds of characteristics and traits make a good leader? Here are some qualities I believe are important: honesty, integrity, commitment, reliability, affability, charisma, intelligence, nobility, compassion, intuition, passion, humility, logic, and organization. They should be soundly professional and have knowledge of organizational management.

Compensation for the leader is set by the board of directors as they consider the budget. Some nonprofit leaders are paid high salaries, but that depends on the size of the organization's budget. For the most part, as the leader, be prepared to negotiate your salary if the offer is lower than you had anticipated, but don't be stunned if the organization is unable to provide the compensation you desire.

DEVELOPMENT DIRECTOR

The development director, if you can hire one, is responsible for fundraising activities and strategies including the solicitation of individuals, major donors, corporations, and foundations. Their knowledge base includes marketing and public relations, grant writing, direct mail solicitation, social events, event planning, sponsorships, database management, the development of planned giving programs, and capital campaigns (to build office space). Also, this person is knowledgeable about diversification of funds.

A good development director's characteristics include the following: compassion, confidence, empathy, affability, authenticity, optimism, organization, reliability and dedication. If this individual performs exceptionally well, then aligning their salary with fundraising contribution is an optional consideration.

As leader, it is up to you to research fair market value for employee salaries. Consider your budget constraints. If you are unable to afford a development director, then the fundraising activities fall on your fundraising skills and abilities. Alternatively, if you cannot afford to hire a development person, create a fundraising committee to recruit individuals who have fundraising experience as volunteers. This is a tactic I used, and the committee outperformed expectations. As you can imagine, their efforts were highly beneficial and appreciated. I recommend that you award the fundraising committee with some form or forms of appreciation such as plaques, socials, or luncheons to demonstrate your gratitude for their service.

BOOKKEEPER OR ACCOUNTANT

I classify this person as the VIP of nonprofits. I cannot stress the importance of having a bookkeeper or accountant on staff. They are responsible for collecting, analyzing, and summarizing accounting information. This person handles or supervises the transactions for paying bills, processing invoices, reconciling accounts, tracking income and expenses and, if applicable, dispensing payroll.

Additionally, they perform bank reconciliations, prepare quarterly financial statements, and assist in audit preparation.

All the tasks are ultimately the responsibility of the leader, but if there is a bookkeeper to perform these activities, the leader is freed up to oversee their performance. Additionally, hiring a bookkeeper allows the leader to work on other aspects of the business.

Characteristics best sought when hiring an accountant or bookkeeper are honesty, integrity, accuracy, organization, precision, and respect. It is also important that the accountant or bookkeeper be methodical and follows standard accounting practice.

How do you pay for a bookkeeper/accountant on a small budget? How expensive are they? Let's say you do not have a budget for an in-house bookkeeper. How about a contractual bookkeeper instead of paying a part-time or full-time bookkeeper? By hiring a contractual bookkeeper to perform basic bookkeeping duties, you will save on payroll insurance and benefits. I suggest that you get three bids from interested bookkeepers and negotiate a price that best fits your organizational budget.

GRANT WRITER

What about grant writing? Professional grant writers can be contractual, as well, which may help to stretch your budget. A good grant writer knows the funding environment and has expertise in pursuing grants on behalf of the organization. The grant writer develops collaborations and partnerships among foundations and corporations. And do not forget that the funds received from the grants can assist in the paying the grant writer. Grant writers add value to the overall management of the business. They save you time, and save the institution money. How? Well, removing grant duties from your desk and giving them to the grant writer gives you more time to work on building collaborations and partnerships.

What characteristics make a good grant writer? Find someone who is enthusiastic, trustworthy, articulate, passionate, realistic, resourceful, and self-reliant.

Before hiring a contractual grant writer, first seek out bids from three grant writers to see what each grant writer offers. For instance, some may only write grants, while others may write grants and meet with corporate leaders to request support. Analyze the grant writer's services and choose the best person without jeopardizing the budget.

PROGRAM MANAGER

Who will administer the programs? If your budget allows, hire a program or project manager. This person will be responsible for administering programs and services. The program manager will manage the day-to-day activities of the program and ensure that the program aligns with the organization's mission statement. This person works closely with the people being served in the program, the volunteers, and management.

Characteristics of a good program manager include the following: compassion, consideration, courtesy, kind-heartedness, empathy, gentleness, and organization.

Compensation is driven by the program requirements. Do you need a part-time program manager or a full-time one? How many people will be served? How many hours per week will it take to serve them? If you serve program recipients within a twenty-hour workweek, then part-time makes sense. You can budget for a part-time program manager. If you are unable to place this person in the budget, recruit a volunteer. Once the program expands financially, then compensation for the program manager would be feasible.

COMMUNICATION MANAGER

How will you market your programs and services? How will you request donations? Most, if not all, businesses and nonprofits market their products or services. And on the wish list of many nonprofit leaders, is the desire for a communication manager or director. A communication manager or marketing director is responsible for promoting the organization through multiple media channels. This person will design and implement public relations and marketing plans. They will also create marketing materials such as e-newsletters, brochures, annual reports, media releases, and donor materials. The communication manager provides publicity through public relations efforts and by building media relations. This person creates website content, performs social media activities, and works closely with production teams to create public service announcements (PSAs).

Characteristics of communication managers include the following: detail orientation, creativity, enthusiasm, faithfulness, honesty, insightfulness, ability to articulate, organization, passion, polish, sympathy, understanding, and well-roundedness.

Compensation for the communication manager depends on how many hours this person will be required to work to complete all aspects of the position. You can start with a part-time communication manager and build up to full-time if the benefits are visible. If you are unable to afford a communication manager, consider creating a communication committee. By now, I am sure you have grasped my theme of using committees wherever and whenever you lack the funds for paid personnel. Volunteers who want to build their communication skills, talents, and experience, tend to volunteer ambitiously on communication committees.

SPECIAL EVENT COORDINATOR/MANAGER

What about a special event coordinator/manager? How can they add value? Special events enhance fundraising efforts. Most organizations host special events to increase donations and awareness. Events introduce the organization to new people and serve to reconnect with ongoing supporters. The event coordinator is responsible for executing strategies related to special events such as galas, festivals, golf tournaments, workshops, seminars, trade shows, walks, tours, and/or VIP events. The coordinator might request or recruit volunteers to assist the implementation of these events. Likewise, your board of directors may contribute in the planning, organizing, and implementation stages of the events.

The following characteristics are needed in a good event coordinator: goal orientation, high energy, ambition, consideration, cooperation, creativity, discipline, the ability to work hard, flexibility, graciousness, innovation, and responsiveness.

Compensation-wise, consider whether you want a paid contractual employee or an unpaid volunteer to handle special events. In contemplating a contractual special event coordinator, budget for a specific time. You may need them for three months or six months depending on the event. If you are working with a committed volunteer in charge of special events—and I say this with zeal—thank the volunteer profusely. You must trust me on this one. There is a lot of work that goes into the planning process, organization, and implementation of a special event. Do not take the hardworking volunteers for granted.

ADMINISTRATIVE SUPPORT PERSON

Who will keep the office running when you are not around? It is great to have an administrative person. If your budget cannot afford administrative staff, the best advice I can share is to recruit a college intern, but remember most interns are searching for something in their field of study. Interns can answer phones, file, greet visitors, perform data entry, conduct research, and perform numerous other duties based on your needs and their interest. Of course, be forewarned that interns come and go every three to five months. Therefore, you must train new interns constantly. Additionally, interns are there to learn and gain valuable experience to improve their résumé. Ask intern candidates what skills they want to develop so you can include assignments that complement their goals and objectives. This gesture will encourage them to perform at a higher level because you have showed concern for their growth. This is the best benefit you can offer to an unpaid intern.

I had an intern interested in mass communications so I included things like writing the e-newsletter, reviewing press releases, and contacting the media to pitch a story in her assignments. Another intern, one who was interested in computer science, received data management assignments. Think of how you can incorporate the intern's interests in the assignments you give them as a way of strengthening their skills and addressing their career aspirations. Adding interns to the staff benefits both the organization and the person working as an intern. I have found it valuable, and I think you will too.

Characteristics of a good administrative support person: capability, courtesy, efficiency, energy, affability, organization, reliability, respect, and self-sufficiency.

Compensation is not required for interns because most are willing to accept unpaid internships to gain the experience and college credit. You will evaluate their performance at the end of the internship or semester as part of their grade. Be sure to review federal Department of Labor rules and regulations on internships to ensure that your intern program complies.

INFORMATION TECHNOLOGY (IT) SPECIALIST

Who will keep your information technology infrastructure operational and secure? IT specialists are experienced in maintaining computer systems, providing technical support, analyzing and solving problems, running system diagnostics, providing a secure network, providing website development, and hosting the organization's domain. As you know, technology networks must function so you can function. The moment your website crashes, or the PayPal function stops working, who can you call?

Characteristics to look for in an IT specialist include the following: knowledge of information systems, honesty, integrity, reliability, dependability, loyalty, confidentiality, responsiveness, skill, and innovativeness.

Where compensation is concerned, try to hire an IT specialist on a retainer basis. You and your board of directors can build this into the budget so you have someone to call if the system crashes, if the internet goes down, if the firewall stops working, or if you have other IT issues and needs. Without an IT person, panic can set in when your system is down or not working optimally. The IT specialist will keep your computers working, your website up, and other aspects of your informational technology infrastructure functioning as they should.

● ● ● ● ● ●

These are the nine critical positions you should fill to achieve your goals in serving the people of your community on little to no budget. Emphasis has been placed on their character because character is extremely important when it comes to serving others. I surrounded myself with people of great character and dynamic characteristics. You should too!

I met and hired the most humane, kind-hearted, generous, dedicated, optimistic, resilient, and sentimental people one could ever encounter. They were stupendous! They had incredible character, and I was honored to work beside them. I have a great admiration and affection for people in the nonprofit sector because most live purpose-driven lives. Luckily, I have seldom found people who were egocentric, narcissistic, arrogant, or insensitive working for charitable organizations. This lucky streak was the best break of my nonprofit career, and I hope you have the same success.

Remember, nobody can do it all. You will need some help. My advice to you is to recruit a solid team to run operations. Even if you must raise the necessary funds to pay staff, commit to doing so. Sufficient staff is needed to accomplish your nonprofits goals and manage its day-to-day affairs.

For the most part, if you don't have adequate funds, then develop a fundraiser to obtain the funds for a contract professional to perform the most critical work and seek enthusiastic volunteers to fill the gaps. Ultimately, you will find that people truly do make the difference.

7

Marketing and Public Relations

MARKETING AND PUBLIC RELATIONS complement each other in nonprofit promotional strategies. Marketing is used to promote products, programs, and services, while public relations concentrates on building awareness of programs and services, and securing positive media attention. Does the organization have a marketing or public relations budget? How much can be devoted to website design and development? What about marketing materials such as brochures and business cards?

When it comes to public relations, the goal is to receive free publicity and positive exposure of your programs, services, and special events at no cost to the organization. Public relations programs allow you to tell your story about the people you serve. That, in turn, will hopefully touch the hearts of donors, potential volunteers, and others who can help you fulfill your organization's mission, thereby changing the lives of those you serve in a positive way.

Undoubtedly, most nonprofits direct their efforts towards free publicity to save money. The media is willing to provide free publicity as a community service, so building media relations is crucial. This is a win-win opportunity for the nonprofit and media.

From annual reports to direct mail campaigns, from social media to public service announcements (PSAs), from speeches to website content, it is basically all about communication channels and promotional materials created to heighten awareness, establish credibility, earn trust, and increase donations. Below is a summary of a few of my favorite public relations (PR) tactics you can incorporate into your promotional mix. You do not need to use them all. Pick and choose the best tactics you believe are achievable. If you are not familiar with the tactics mentioned below, search the web for examples.

ANNUAL REPORTS

Your staff or you can produce annual reports to inform stakeholders about the activities and financial position of your organization. The annual report can be as brief as four pages. It may be in print form, printable electronic form, or both. Inside the annual report, demonstrate to your stakeholders how their investment in the organization has helped program recipients receive the necessary services to improve their qualities of life. Make sure you have the metrics, and don't leave anything out. In other words, let stakeholders know the exact number of clients served. For example, if you served four thousand people through your soup kitchen program; or five hundred homeless individuals received temporary transitional housing, give the numbers, don't overstate or understate them, give the exact number you served. Also show your stakeholders the impact of their in-kind and cash donations.

AUDIO NEWS RELEASES

The audio news release (ANR) is generally a promotional spot for radio that is fifteen to thirty seconds long. You create soundbites about the organization itself or special event taking place. You can be the spokesperson or you can have a volunteer, someone from the board, or talent from the radio station record the announcement. An ANR should be free for nonprofits; but some radio stations aiming to increase their revenue may wish to charge you. Save money by inquiring about radio station sponsorship of your ANR. Seek out and try to establish rapport with a local radio station that best fits your targeted demographics of donors and supporters.

BILLBOARDS AND OUT-OF-HOME ADVERTISEMENTS

Perhaps you want to elevate the organization to another level by using billboards and out-of-home advertisements found on buses and other transit systems. Research advertising companies about this kind of advertising, know costs involved, and evaluate your options. You must aim for a good return on investment (ROI). In other words, make sure there are measurable results for the money you dispense for this style of advertising. You do not want to waste the organization's money.

BLOGS

If you are ecstatic about blogging and have ample time to attend to your blog, then blog on. Blogging is a dynamic communication channel you can use to enlighten your clientele and supporters about a topic you choose for the day, week, or month. It takes discipline to maintain your blogging site to keep your target audience returning again and again. Make sure you have the time to blog.

BROCHURES

I find brochures to be effective for spreading the word. Make brochures aesthetically pleasing to the eyes and full of vibrant colors and graphics. Include artwork that grabs the reader's attention. Make brochures interactive by adding a short survey or call to action at the end. As an example, let's say you want to understand why someone would support your program. A short survey with three to five questions may help you evaluate the effectiveness of your programs. At the same time, it allows the individual to interact with the organization in an insightful manner.

Another way to make brochures interactive is to include a donation form at the back. You will be pleasantly surprised when the form returns with a generous donation from a supporter.

Always include the most pertinent information in your brochures: mission statement, logo, phone, address, e-mail, website, how to donate, and/how to get involved. To save on production costs, create the brochures in-house using publishing software and find a local printing company to print the brochures pro bono.

DIRECT MAIL CAMPAIGNS

When initiating a direct mail campaign to reach your supporters or target audience for donations, decide how often you want to implement the campaign. Review your financial statements. Do you see any months without incoming funds? If so, your low-income months would be ideal times of the year to employ a direct mail campaign. Direct mail requires a good mailing list of your supporters. You may have five thousand supporters in the database system. If you have that many supporters, do what I did. I initiated four separate direct mail campaigns to target one-fourth of the contributors every quarter. I did this for two reasons: I had a small staff, and I did not want to bombard supporters with several mailings throughout the year. At times, the donations received from direct mail campaigns were minimal. Because of that, I recommend that you break down the campaign into sections versus dispensing an enormous amount of time and energy all at one time for a potentially small return.

DONATED MEDIA

Saving your budget is essential, so donated media are favored by nonprofits seeking to stretch their promotional and marketing dollars. Donated media take the form of a public service announcement (PSA), which the organization does not pay for because a radio or television sponsor runs the PSAs pro bono. Free advertisement is the best. The only drawback is that you have no control over the time of day a spot airs. Nevertheless, rest assured, someone is watching your spot—even in the middle of the night.

E-MAIL MARKETING

E-mail marketing works well with a well-orchestrated plan. If you have supporters' eager to become engaged with your mission, collect their e-mails and use e-mail marketing to invite them to participate in various activities and special events. E-mail marketing can keep supporters informed of what is happening within your organization. E-mail marketing targets devoted supporters to communicate with them on a regular basis.

MEDIA KIT

A media kit is a promotional folder that introduces your organization to the media. If you connect with reporters frequently or aspire
to attract media attention, preparing a media kit may be worth your
time. Include backgrounders (history of organization or issue), fact
sheets, frequently asked questions (FAQs), contact information, and
any pertinent information that collectively elevates your organization and makes it newsworthy. The best way to use a media kit is to
send it directly to interested reporters to introduce your organization to them with hopes of gaining their interest in news coverage.

MEDIA RELEASES

Media releases—also called news releases and press releases—are
the most popular and effective public relations tool used for mass
communication sent to the media, be it newspaper, radio, television, or internet. Media releases attract media attention and recog-
nition. When composing media releases, it is crucial to be factual.
There is no need for glitz and glitter. Just state the facts. Don't jeop-
ardize, impede, or damage your credibility or reputation with the
media by using hyperbole or otherwise misrepresenting the facts.

    If you are unfamiliar with how to write a media release, I
strongly suggest you learn the correct way to write one before sending it off. If you are well versed on how to write them, I recommend
that you always have someone else review them before sending
them out. You will have to trust me on this when I say that it will
save you from the embarrassment of including misspellings, awkward phrases, and incorrect or inappropriate words.

NEWSLETTERS OR E-NEWSLETTERS

You can produce a monthly or quarterly newsletter or e-newsletter to inform donors about how their donations have been used and news about your organization and its activities. Add compelling personal stories about those served by donations. Assign this task to your communications staff, volunteer, or committee if your schedule does not allow you to create it personally. Your newsletter does not have to be elaborate or voluminous. Something short and concise works. Newsletters allow supporters to stay well-informed about programs, the direction of the organization, changes in leadership, and, how the organization is changing lives thanks to their generous giving.

Although readers may only glance through articles, newsletters can provide a continual connection and build an affinity to the organization.

PSAs AND VNRs

The public service announcement (PSA) is the best visual public relations tool to promote controlled messages, even though you cannot control when the PSA will air. As mentioned above in the donated media section, to produce a PSA, establish a good working relationship with a production company or the media. Depending on the group you work with, you may have to write the script or discuss your concept with a producer. PSAs add value and credibility to your organization.

A video news release (VNR) can also be independently produced by a television sponsor to save your budget. VNRs work well for reporters needing a story that will take up two or three minutes of air time. Some VNRs can be up to ten minutes in length, and they can focus on one or two elements, such as programs and/or people served. If the VNR is professionally produced, you can place it on your website for additional exposure.

SOCIAL MEDIA

Social media encompasses several online communication channels like Facebook, LinkedIn, Twitter, YouTube, and many others. You can incorporate these channels into your marketing and public relations tactics.

Facebook

Facebook is beneficial for promoting special events or to share photos from a recent event. Your supporters may post photos or comments about your special event, gala, or golf tournament. It is self-promotion that works well whenever you have something positive to share with the community.

LinkedIn

LinkedIn is a social media platform you can use to inform your colleagues and followers of volunteer opportunities, board openings, and other opportunities for involvement with your organization. LinkedIn is also good for connecting with professionals in your area.

Twitter

Twitter is a good social networking tool for quick messages about the organization. Be aware that the messages should be controlled by internal personnel. The tweets should be clear, concise, and completely professional in nature. They should contain positive comments about the organization. You can even use Twitter to give congratulations and special thanks.

YouTube

YouTube is an incredible video-based social media outlet you can use to highlight your programs, clients, services, and the work you do in the community. While it does not take a full-blown production company to create a YouTube video, try to have it professionally produced to better reflect your organization's image. Videos on YouTube can be seen by anyone, including the media. Place your YouTube video links on your website for more visibility.

SPECIAL EVENTS

Special events such as galas, 5k walks or runs, golf tournaments, product launches, and VIP events bring substantial financial support to your organization. Special events increase awareness of your programs and increase revenues. Keep in mind that special events expend human resources to the greatest limit. Choose the event or events suitable for the amount of staff and volunteers you recruit to plan, organize, coordinate, and implement them.

TALK SHOWS

Promotions through television and radio talk shows offer an opportunity to talk about the uniqueness of your charitable organization. Study your market. Find radio and television stations that offer talk-show formatted programs highlighting the work of nonprofits. Talk shows offer you the opportunity to talk in-depth about the work you do for the community. If given the chance to be on a talk show, take it.

TRADE SHOWS

The key to trade shows is having an attractive exhibit to lure visitors to your booth so you can educate them about your products and services. Components of that exhibit might include brochures, marketing products (pens, wristbands, calendars, etc.), full-color banner, a table (if not provided), a tablecloth, table signage, fliers, and other materials specific to your organization. Attempt to fill your table with promotional items, and allow visitors to easily access them. Be accessible and engaging. Try standing in front of your booth to welcome your guests and answer any questions they have.

WEBSITE CONTENT

First impressions are paramount! Your website must capture your visitor's attention. If it does not, your visitor may exit swiftly. Have your website professionally developed. Although cost can be a factor, raising funds for an efficient and effective website is well worth it. Website content must be created and kept fresh. For newly created sites, your communication staff must generate enough content for each web page. Admittedly, writing can be time consuming, and if you do not have a writer on staff, consider asking interns, volunteers, or board members to write the content.

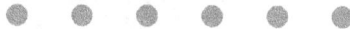

●　　●　　●　　●　　●　　●

I have given you numerous marketing and public relations vehicles and tools. You will probably not use all of them. Use the ones that best work for your target audience. Remember, the main objective of marketing and public relations is to increase awareness and visibility. No organization has unlimited funds for marketing campaigns or public relations activities. Use the funds you do have wisely to highlight your organization's uniqueness and to introduce your products and services to those who may be unaware of them, and capitalize on donated media and other free vehicles.

Without question, developing effective marketing and public relations campaigns takes time, expertise, and funds of all involved—you, your development director and/or communications manager (if you have one or both), and that of other staff members. If you want your organization to thrive and the people you serve to benefit, the world should know about your worthy cause. And when the world does, your efforts will prove themselves worth it.

8

Putting Systems in Place

N O NONPROFIT ORGANIZATION CAN operate in both an effective and efficient way without systems. Just as systems are needed in the for-profit world, they are also needed in the nonprofit world.

If you are hired into a leadership position for a nonprofit organization that already has standard operating procedures (SOP) in place, great! If not, it is a good idea to create an SOP manual. I had no standard operating procedures when I stepped into my role as executive director of a nonprofit, but little by little, I discovered procedures that needed to be part of the overall organizational structure.

For instance, accounting practices and procedures were different from other organizations because of the nature of the organization and the people being served. Grants were distributed monthly as part of the program. Financial management and oversight included methods of tracking monthly expenses. Networking and community connections needed to be captured because it took years to build those relationships and I did not want to lose them. By placing important names and contact information in the SOP, the next executive leader or inevitable successor would know who to start with to maintain those valuable relationships.

Place anything you think of that is unique to your organization in your SOP. I prefer to think of the SOP as a good road map the next leader can use to take the journey through the organization's files. As a matter of fact, it will save them immeasurable time because they will not have to read every file on a computer that may house thousands of documents. They will just simply pick up the SOP manual and carry on business as usual. Therefore, fundraising will not suffer nor the business operations. The SOP manual will be one of their most valuable tools.

CREATING AN SOP MANUAL

When you are creating an SOP manual, consider having procedures for the following in it:
✓   Accounting/Financial Management
✓   Business Operations
✓   Fundraising/Special Events
✓   Governance
✓   Grants
✓   Human Resources
✓   IT/Website
✓   Marketing Strategies
✓   Programs
✓   Strategic Planning

- ✓ Partnerships/Collaborations
- ✓ Forms
- ✓ Passwords

ACCOUNTING/FINANCIAL MANAGEMENT

Current accounting policies and operating procedures used on a daily, weekly, and monthly basis should be included in an SOP manual. Add information you receive from your CPA. Place the most current audit and the 990 in this section and update it annually. Also, it is a good idea to include a copy of Form 941 Employer's Quarterly Federal Tax Return. The accounting section will be useful as a reference during your next audit.

You may want to include information about bill processing, making deposits, processing donations, accounts payable, accounts receivable, business credit card usage, and how to process credit cards. Don't forget to add information specific to the documents you need to file annually with your state. The office of your Secretary of State will have annual filing instructions and business renewal deadlines.

BUSINESS OPERATIONS

Do you know when your building lease is about to expire? Place a copy of the current lease agreement and information on when the lease will expire in your SOP manual. The business operations section should outline rent/lease payments.

Does your organization belong to community groups? Do you have to renew memberships? Be sure to add information about group memberships, including renewal dates and if your organization pays for renewals or the staff members pay for group membership renewals themselves.

You may have special accounts for office equipment such as the phone system, postage meter, and printers, and for website maintenance. You should place account information for all of this in the business operations section.

FUNDRAISING/SPECIAL EVENTS

Nonprofit organizations thrive on fundraising. In this section of the SOP manual, include the events calendar, which lists every event that the organization holds. This will help in the planning, coordination, and management of all events throughout the year. For major fundraising events, such as galas or walks, include the event checklist indicating the tasks and activities involved in the event. Additionally, provide the contact information of the top volunteers for those events. Continuity of volunteers leads to a successful event because they know what to do and when.

GOVERNANCE

Every nonprofit should have articles of incorporation, a board of directors list, bylaws, a certificate of exemption, strategic plans, IRS letter of determination or 501(c)3, a mission statement, along with policies that relate to the board, such as a conflict of interest policy, a document retention policy, and a whistleblower policy. Place these documents under governance.

GRANTS

In this section, identify the grants to apply for, the names of the granting organizations, contact information, grant year dates, and application deadlines. You may also want to include a copy of the latest grant written that followed the grant writing guidelines described in Chapter 2. This way the latest cover letter, narrative, and attachments are available for creating future grant proposals.

HUMAN RESOURCES

If you have a staff and do not have an employee handbook, create one. In the employee handbook, describe your legal obligations as an employer and what their employee rights are; it should include policies on work hours, standards of conduct, probationary periods, termination, and resignation procedures. You should also have an Occupational Safety and Health Administration (OSHA) compliance policy, a nondisclosure agreement, antidiscrimination policies, and Equal Employment Opportunity (EEO) statement. Also include workers compensation and harassment issues. A summary of employee benefits should also be in the manual with details relating to time off and family medical leave.

Each employee is required to sign an Employee Eligibility Verification Form I-9 that you, as the employer, will keep on file.

One great resource I used to help me create my employee handbook is the Small Business Administration site (www.SBA.gov). It outlines what you should include in your employee handbook.

IT/WEBSITE

In this section, you can list who currently hosts the organization's website, along with their contact information, as well as who created the most recent version of the website. Websites need maintenance, security checks, and updates. Ensure that information is included about the maintenance schedule.

MARKETING STRATEGIES

Are there any marketing restrictions outlined by the board of directors? This is a good section to list any policies and procedures relating to marketing the organization. You may also want to add examples of the marketing materials produced, such as brochures, business cards, and letterhead. Who do you order these supplies from? Also, if you have any special marketing accounts with Facebook, Twitter, Webmail, or other companies, place the account information in this section.

PROGRAMS

Your unique program serves hundreds and thousands in your community. In this section describe how your program is structured, how program recipients apply for your services, and how the program is administered. This information is helpful for your board of directors and anyone in charge of managing the programs of the organization.

STRATEGIC PLANNING

The good news about strategic plans is that your board or former leader probably already devised a plan. If that is the case, I highly suggest you do the happy dance! Strategic planning takes time to create, coordinate, manage, organize, implement, and evaluate. Your organization needs to identify where you have been and where you are going. The plan should outline how you are going to get there.

If you need help in creating a strategic plan, know that there are numerous books about strategic planning, especially relating to nonprofit organizations. I think the best strategic plans are only two or three pages—something manageable.

PARTNERSHIPS/COLLABORATIONS

Do you know who your coalition partners are? What organizations are doing the same thing you do? Who has your organization collaborated with? List the partnerships developed that have been beneficial to the organization and with whom you want to maintain strong relations. Provide names and contact information. Update both on a regular basis.

FORMS

I'm guessing that not everyone is a form fanatic like me. I created a form for just about everything except how many times to snack during the day. Create a forms section in your SOP manual. You may want to include the annual fund letter (to send out to donors), credit card processing forms (for donations received via phone), new employee checklist, reimbursement form, thank you letter format, time off form, and volunteer information form.

PASSWORDS

Passwords and PIN numbers for computer logins, credit cards, and bank accounts should be kept confidential. Lock them away or store them in a secure location. However, the board president should be aware of where to locate this information in the event you are not available or you leave the organization.

• • • • • •

By putting systems in place and constructing a standard operating procedures manual, you will establish continuity within the structure of the organization. Your inevitable successor or board member will not only appreciate the attention you have given to systems and procedures, they will find their integration into the organization much easier because of it. Systems help keep an organization operating with the fewest interruptions, and the time you take to create them will end up saving you time in the long run.

9

The Fun

I ENJOY PLAYING AS much as I enjoy working, but my mother taught me that I must get my chores done before I can go out and play. In the world of nonprofits, as well as the for-profit world, that translates to business before pleasure. The problem with that approach is that it is very easy to find so many business responsibilities to keep you occupied that you may never feel able to play or have any kind of fun without feeling guilt.

If you have stepped into a leadership role at a nonprofit you have by now probably attended to all or most of the things covered thus far, from getting to know the organization and its people to digging into fundraising and from engaging the board of directors to creating standard operating procedures.

Whew! The day-to-day operations can wear you out. So, what's next? Playtime. That's where you, as a leader, must stop and take time to do something playful and fun. Why? Because your effectiveness as a leader will deteriorate and your health might even suffer if you do not fold in some playtime.

How did this playtime come about for me? One morning, I woke up feeling unbelievably ill. My head was throbbing, I had blurred vision, and I was experiencing heart palpitations. I had aches and pains in my back, shoulders, neck, and feet, and I felt dire melancholy. I knew my weekly chores, along with long hours, were to blame for my declining health. Even worse, I felt awful for being sick. All I could think about were the sixty or more e-mails waiting for my answer, the meetings I needed to schedule, the report that had to go out, and the grant that was due the next day. I wondered how I could possibly serve the people counting on me if I couldn't get out of bed.

As I grabbed the side of the bed and slowly pulled myself up to what I viewed as the reality of my responsibilities, my husband glanced over at me and said, "Where are you going?"

"To work," I replied. "I have a lot of work ahead of me."

He shook his head in disbelief. "What happens if you don't go to work today? Is the job more important than your health?"

Another reality check slapped me in the face.

It was a good question. Is your job more important than your health?

It is not uncommon for leaders to fall victim to overworking—to working long hours, nonstop, trying to secure yet another thousand dollars, trying to keep programs running smoothly, and trying to keep the organization as a whole viable. Then the leader finds that her body, mind, and soul turn against her. And what about her family? If she has placed her job higher than them on the scale of importance, have they turned against her too? If not, will they?

Before you become ill, before your mind stops working for you reliably, and before you feel your soul has been sucked right out of your body, purposely add fun into your life. Stop doing chores and take time off. Whether you think you need it or not, I recommend that you take time for yourself. You are not benefiting yourself, the organization, your family, or your friends if you work to the point of severe burnout.

I stopped, I looked at how I had inadvertently fallen into a pattern of overwork, and I listened to the pleas of my family. I made changes and sought out fun activities instead of "fund" activities.

Let's face it; being in charge, being the leader responsible for the successes and failures of an organization, can be stressful, challenging, and rewarding. And it comes with a price. If you're wearing several hats, there will be times when you're ready to give up, simply because the challenges and stress feel bigger than your ability to handle them. During my personal journey through executive leadership, I found fun activities that kept me going when the stress barometer reached the highest levels, and I'm going to share them with you.

First, you should switch from the executive mindset to the fun mindset. It's time to think differently, renew your spirit, and find happiness by doing something new and vivacious. Then stop spending twelve to sixteen hours a day working and start getting into life. I know how easy it is to forget about the other part of life—family, friends, and children, but if you do not reclaim some hours and trim your workload, you may find yourself in bed one day, like me, realizing that overwork has stripped you of your power to lead—or even follow a trail of breadcrumbs back to the office. You're in charge! It's time to act like it.

THE FUN FACTOR

To renew your spirits and shift from overworking to living life more fully, the magic ingredient is the fun factor. Here are some tips for you to peruse. Pick the ones you feel like having fun with. Embrace the newness, relieve the stress, and start to play.

Health and Happiness

What would happen if you lost your health today or tomorrow? Could the work of the organization continue without you? I bring these questions up because we often think we're indispensable. We focus on the work in front of us and forget to take care of ourselves. My best advice is this: exercise, exercise, exercise. If you exercise even two or three times a week for thirty minutes each exercise period, you are helping to prevent what is known as the "executive heart attack." I haven't had one, but there have been times when my chest was so tight from tension and anxiety buildup, the pressure seemed like a heart attack. Exercise helped relieve the stress and pressure. Choose exercise you enjoy, like bike riding, walking, or swimming.

Children, Pets, and Young People

Have you ever sat and watched how children, pets, and young people play? You will be surprised by how humorously they present themselves. Surround yourself with laughter. If your children are small, you already know how funny they are, naturally. They trigger laughter on sight. Savor those moments. If you are a pet lover, spend quality time with your pet through walks in the park. Cherish the tail wags after they've done something wrong, thinking they were right. Teens and young adults offer intriguing conversations and an array of perspectives about life in today's world. They often tell stories that are comical and bring laughter and joy to your life. Laugh on.

Music

I wish I could say I'm a musician. I'm not. I read sheet music and love to play the piano to relieve stress and anxiety. I can play for hours learning a new piece. Music—from smooth jazz to soft contemporary—can relax you and bring your body and mind to a calm state. Try working with soft background music playing on your computer. Close your office door and put the Do Not Disturb sign out while listening to your favorite music. Music contributes to mental health, happiness, and joy. If the music moves you, sway with it or dance.

Sports

Whether it is tennis, baseball, golf, football, soccer, or some other sport, celebrate your successes by taking time to play your favorite sport. When I realized that I was working constantly—long hours, weekends, and even some holidays—and had built-up a pool of vacation days I dishonored by not tapping into, I began to see that I was doing tremendous damage to my body and mind. Adding play-time made a world of difference in my attitude, strength, endurance, and stability.

Smile While Speaking

As an optimist, I have carried positive thoughts and a positive attitude throughout my life. My family, friends, and associates are quick to point out that I am always smiling.

I also speak on the phone with a smile in my voice, a skill I learned when I worked for a large Fortune 500 company in the sales division. One sales person always brightened my day whenever I spoke to her on the phone. Every time she called, her smile radiated through the phone like sunshine beaming on an ocean. I decided to cherish that characteristic and make it my personal trademark. My best advice to you, especially during those unbelievably high stress days, is to maintain a smile and a positive attitude. I know it can be difficult on those days when you want to curse at everyone, but believe me when I say that it works. Remain positive, remain optimistic, and smile.

Give Yourself Kudos

On any given Friday, if I hadn't accomplished everything I intended in my role as leader, I felt like a failure. One day I realized it is more important to celebrate your successes than chastising yourself for everything not yet accomplished. What did you accomplish today? Kudos to you! It doesn't matter what you didn't finish. Celebrate the projects you did complete.

I once answered twenty e-mails out of a hundred and celebrated the accomplishment of answering those twenty e-mails. I decided to celebrate the next twenty answered and the twenty after that, too. After you realize that you simply cannot do it all, that working until midnight to answer all one hundred e-mails is not worth it, you will begin to understand and appreciate what you *can* complete. Therefore, feel no shame. Save some for another day. My husband has pointed out that if it is important, they will call, not send an e-mail.

Love Being a Philanthropist

If you are a nonprofit leader, you are a philanthropist. You give of your time and your money. Becoming a philanthropist is fun, heartwarming, and uplifting. You give to the causes that matter the most to you. You know you're making a difference within your organization and the many other organizations you support. You know you're impacting the lives of people within your local community and beyond. You know the power of the dollar. Don't stop giving. As a leader, you are a shining star in your community because of your unwavering passion.

Spirits Up

Think about what kind of drink makes you happy. Is it a smoothie, herbal tea, or a health drink? Maybe you prefer wine, beer, or a margarita. You will notice that I chose drinks, not food. The reason is that whenever I feel overwhelmed, I drink something that is both fun and healthy. Choose whatever works for you without overindulging. The object is to brighten up your day and lift your spirits on those incredibly horrible days. If food is used as stress relief, easy does it. Gaining weight will only add to stress. Avoid sweets and snacking all day—I'm speaking from experience and my scale on that—and watch portion size at dinner time.

Travel to Neverland

As an executive, when was the last time you took a vacation or went on a nonbusiness trip? I am often reminded that traveling to see relatives is not a real vacation, but I throw those trips in from time to time. I suggest you take a vacation.

I found it easy to continue working for months without ever taking time off. There is so much to be done in way of fundraising and development, and who will do the work if you're not around? Who will oversee the operation? Of course, this is where that dynamic word "delegate" comes into play. Delegate projects to your staff, board of directors, or volunteers and go somewhere—anywhere. Travel to an exotic island or play golf in different states. Do something new and different. If you have friends you haven't seen in years, give them a call and tell them you're on your way. Escape for a moment. You will return to work refreshed and rejuvenated. Your thinking will be clearer and crisper. You may even find that your personal wisdom quotient has gone up a few notches because you have returned to a state of congruency—and when that happens, both you and the organization benefit.

Out to Lunch

You have lunch with co-workers, associates, board members, community leaders, and other leaders. Switch it up! Call your spouse or a close friend and schedule a long lunch. Call two, four, or ten of your friends and invite them to a Saturday lunch or Sunday brunch. It's great to congregate with friends. The trick to lunch is to schedule a lunch outing with the vow to discuss something other than work. Talk about children, football, politics, movies, the latest technology, or bad hair days—anything but work.

The Power of No

I know many of you have heard this one before: Just say no. Throughout my career, I served on numerous boards and committees—so many, in fact, that exhaustion became my middle name and my never ending, crazed schedule became too much. I learned the power of no. Learn to say no politely to anyone and everyone who is demanding of your time. Free your time to do other things you really enjoy, whether that is crafts, gardening, visiting friends, or any other pastime. Avoid overcommitting yourself and reserve your energy.

Classes with Zing

I found solace and fun in cooking classes. For you it may be swimming, gardening, kayaking, fishing, hang-gliding, rock climbing, hiking, golfing, or bowling. Find a class that takes you away from the normal routine. Maybe it is something that will challenge your mind in a different way. I know I mentioned cooking, which is classified as normal activity in most households, but it is anything but normal in mine. I only cooked on occasions until I took a cooking class. Now I enjoy experimenting to witness my husband's reaction. Although I'm not convinced he is enjoying the experimentation—though I certainly am—he always has a reaction.

Socializing with Friends and Family

Another method of relieving stress and having fun is to socialize with friends and family. This can be as simple as a Friday evening cocktail hour or going over to a family member's home to kick back and relax—without talking about work. This seems to be highly difficult for people to do if they have had a hectic workweek and are ready to throw their hands in the air. They need to vent. If that is you, find other ways to let off steam and regain your composure—perhaps a combination of exercise and meditation—but avoid bringing it into your time with friends and family. Socializing with friends and family reconnects you with what is important and inserts a bit of that fun factor into your life.

● ● ● ● ● ●

The fun factor should not be overlooked. Not only will it help recharge your batteries, but it will help keep your mind, body, spirit, and emotions in harmony. As a result, your effectiveness as a leader will be enhanced. The incredible demands of being a leader in the nonprofit world can contribute to health problems. Some days can be overwhelming. Most days will require your full presence and long work hours. To retain the harmony that is critical to both your health and your effectiveness as a leader, you must know when to turn the work off. Make the time to play.

THE DUH IN FUN-DUH-MENTAL

To be a fun-duh-mental leader and not just a fundamental leader requires acknowledging that you do not and cannot know everything. Is it possible for a leader to have the answers to every question and every problem? No. I don't know anyone in this world who knows everything.

That is where the "duh" comes into play. And I used the word "play" here deliberately because once you abandon the belief that you can know everything, everything lightens up and you can allow yourself to be playful about your humanness while simultaneously being serious about your work and your organization's mission.

As a leader of a nonprofit organization, you are expected to learn everything you can about the organization, but you may not have the answer to every question asked by donors, staff, board members, program recipients, marketing teams, IT professionals, or the media. Be well versed on the organization's history and its founder. Read the articles of incorporation thoroughly. Have a firm grasp of the strategic/business plan, the financials, operations, fundraising, and the other aspects of the organization you, as leader, are expected to know. But never think you can know everything.

Revel in the information others in your organization have that you don't because the nonprofit is stronger with the collective knowledge of staff and volunteers. It is a great deal more fun to work with a team who understands the power of the whole than it is to work with the misguided belief that you, as leader, must carry the load for the entire team.

Here are the crucial qualities of being a leader: decision-making expertise and problem-solving ability. You do not have all the answers. If you cannot answer a question posed by your board, your donors, your staff, or those you serve, admit it. Then set about finding the answer.

And while you are getting that answer, remind yourself that allowing yourself to be fully human is a lot more fun than pretending you are perfect and have all the answers. It makes you more fun to work with, too.

10

The Mental

I CANNOT TELL YOU how many times you will need a mental break from the never-ending mental challenges of problem solving for a nonprofit. It is the job that never sleeps. Situations arise beyond your control. Your mind will constantly work through the night creating campaigns, preparing reports, reenacting staff problems and concerns, and thinking of how and what you're going to say the next morning. You never stop raising money in your head and you never stop solving problems. The wheels never stop turning. Your mind becomes overly stressed. You will need a mental break.

TACTICS FOR STAYING SANE

Conflicts, disagreements, and interruptions at work create high anxiety. Rushing to complete projects causes stressful circumstances. The lack of spending precious time with family and friends can lead to guilty feelings and mental anguish. As leaders, we need mental breaks.

Beyond taking breaks, there are several things you can do to stay sane and avoid overtaxing the mental part of being a fun-duh-mental leader.

Conflict

I prefer little to no confrontation because conflicts waste valuable time when there is so much work to be done within the organization. Employees are entitled to complain and have differences of opinions and beliefs. Some believe they are treated unfairly. Some like to complain about everything. Some argue with other employees for no clear reason. Some want to file a formal complaint and bring in legal counsel due to irreconcilable differences. Whatever the issue, people react to situations that are disturbing to them.

But when conflicts or disputes arise, it is best to negotiate and resolve them quickly so they don't linger and start to erode the fabric of the organization. Make sure that employee handbook you created has policies that protect the organization and employee rights. If it does not, create those policies so everyone in the organization has guidance and rules on performance and behavior.

Meditation

Relax. Meditation is the best method to relax your mind, body and soul. If you are at work, close your door, turn off the lights, close your eyes, and breathe deep. Be in peace and quiet for a few minutes without thinking about work. Clear your mind. Don't say a word. Listen to the quiet. Listen to your breathing and just relax. Meditation is a method that all too often people forget about, yet it is one of the most effective rejuvenating activities one can do. Try it, you will be re-energized.

Massage

Why not get a massage? A massage may be the answer to relieving any tension headache or muscle ache. This is another way to clear your thoughts. A soothing massage while listening to calm musical tunes will put you in a relaxation state of mind. Tell your massage therapist if you are experiencing any back pain, muscle cramps, or shoulder or neck pain. Their expertise will help diminish your aches and pains. The relaxation feeling from a massage will last for hours. This is a fabulous way to destress your mind.

Honey, I'm Home

Go home. Relationships must never be forgotten. I spoke about this earlier and am emphasizing it again because it is critical, and you can learn from my mistakes. When your spouse, children, or other family members need attention, find a way to give it to them. I know how important it is to hold on to a job, especially if it's a job as a leader and holds great promise. But I can also promise you that if the job takes precedence over everyone else in your life, relationships can be damaged—sometimes beyond repair.

It will not only benefit your relationships with family members to spend time with them, but it will also save more than a few mental gray cells. If you are concerned about your family, you cannot be your best at work, and if you are concerned about your work, you cannot be your best with your family. When you go home, be at home.

Close the Door

You're an executive; you're going to be interrupted frequently. There is no way around it, but there are some things you can do about it. Close your door and place a Do Not Disturb sign on it. It doesn't always work. Someone is bound to knock on your door and apologize for disturbing you because they want an answer to whether you want pink or purple as the primary color theme for the upcoming fundraiser gala. When that happens, use it as an opportunity to again explain your closed-door policy to your staff: When the door is closed, it means to hold all calls and all questions unless they impact the bottom line or relate a true emergency. Executives need to concentrate on important projects without interruptions. Employees need to understand that the main fundraiser and strategic visionary of the organization needs concentration time.

Get the Facts from Other Leaders

Meet with others in your shoes to discuss challenges and how they handle them. When I first took over as a nonprofit executive, I met with numerous leaders and probed their minds about best practices and how to stay on top of everything, since the number of hats I was wearing could have filled a millinery shop. Some of their advice resonated quite nicely. Of course, some possessed the advantage of having more staff, but I incorporated some of their suggestions to make my life easier. For instance, one executive warned about overscheduling meetings throughout the workday and how it caused high anxiety for her when she did overschedule because she inevitably fell behind on all the administrative duties that come with the job. So, I immediately stopped scheduling four to five meetings a day.

Live Below Your Means

Nonprofit leaders may not be paid as high as private leaders, but for the most part, they can earn a decent living. One trick I learned is to live below my means. Okay, I admit that when I worked for private industry, having a Mercedes and Lexus in the garage seemed appropriate. But what about having a high-end luxury car when you are trying to raise money for low income individuals or the homeless? How does that look?

Image is important when you are trying to convey your message to anyone you are approaching for donations. If you are wealthy and working as a nonprofit leader, then be one of your organization's top funders if you can.

If you are earning a decent salary, keep in mind that as with any job, it may not last. Living below your means may allow you to maintain a good quality of life if your great job disappears and it takes you a while to find your next creative engagement. If you have a spouse or significant other making a substantial salary, take the opportunity to save money, invest in real estate, or place more money away in your 401k. As an executive, you never know how or when the wind will shift. My best advice is to be prepared.

Become Debt Free

Become debt free, at least where your credit cards are concerned. My husband and I paid off one credit card at a time. There are numerous books on how to pay down your debt. I like paying one at a time because if I have applied $75 a month to credit card number one and eventually pay it off, I can next apply that same $75 to credit card number two, adding that money to the $40 a month I have been paying on it. That $115 will now increase the speed at which I pay off credit card number two. It is a proven method that has worked not only for credit cards, but car payments as well. Your house may be another story, but if you have the system in place, you can pay off your house faster too.

Dealing with Difficult People

If you have been in the workplace for long, you will have encountered difficult people of one kind or another. It is as inevitable as fluctuations in the stock market and can be equally unsettling. There will always be people who do not think like you and you may even encounter people who are determined to prove you wrong. Maybe you work with people who talk down to you or belittle you, or maybe you know people who are narcissistic and only think of themselves. They do exist.

I suggest that you be patient with them, find common ground, avoid conflict, and take the time to communicate with them to better understand why they think the way they do. If you are the leader working with subordinates who want to disobey your directives, take the time to explain your expectations. If you must take disciplinary action, make sure you are clear about what changes they may need to make. You can then monitor their performance over the next thirty days for behavioral changes. The objective is to give them a clear understanding of what is required and create documentation should you need to dismiss the employee or need a paper trail during an employee dispute.

Make It a Fantastic Day

You control your mind. Create in your mind how your fantastic day looks, even if you must pretend you get the big grant award you wanted. Wouldn't that make your day? Smile. Run with those thoughts and make it a great day. The power of positive thinking stirs motivation. Your day will flow better.

Thank Volunteers

Thank your volunteers and staff often. Remember, you cannot carry on the work of the organization without them. They chose the nonprofit world because they care, and they chose your nonprofit because they care about the mission. They are working for you to help you reach your goals. Volunteers are working for free, and unfortunately, due to some low-wages in the nonprofit sector, staff members are *almost* working for free, so treat them all with dignity and respect. Take them to lunch, provide a thank you card, or purchase a gift basket of goodies. Show some appreciation for the work they do. By showing your appreciation, they will be honored to work with you and continue working on behalf of the people your organization serves. Thank them often; it is a refreshing mental break for you and them.

Family Counts the Most

Don't forget to thank your family often. They endure your long hours of work. Whether you have been attending fundraising events at night or finishing a work project during the weekend, you can thank your family by taking them to dinner, to a movie, bowling, or out for game night— anything to show your appreciation of their continued support. Your relationship with them will grow stronger because you're giving them the attention they want and deserve.

Get Organized

How do you stay organized? It's tough, but being organized relieves stress. If you strive to always have blank file folders and labels near your desk, you can quickly file stuff away. Place anything you print out into a folder immediately. Avoid stacks of work on your desk. File as you go through your day or delegate to others. If you walk into your office and there are documents everywhere, it's time for you to take control. Come in on the weekend and file everything away or otherwise put things in order. A cluttered desk leads to a cluttered mind.

Go to Lunch Alone

Relief can come in the form of escape. Whenever my day became too challenging and overwhelming, when I could not meet everyone's demands—from being at every meeting requested to completing the IRS forms and from paying the operational bills to responding to the flood of e-mails in my inbox—escaping from the drudgery brought much needed relief. Sometimes nice walks, a drive to a nearby park, or browsing through a book store did the trick.

Hangout Buddy

Whenever you become exhausted from working tedious hours, call on your hangout buddy and go to a local club, pub, restaurant, or shopping center. Go have your favorite drink. Get on the dance floor and cut loose, and if you don't know how to dance, cut loose anyway. Laugh at yourself. You will be surprised by how much tension disappears.

● ● ● ● ● ●

I have only briefly touched about how to relieve mental stress. If I gathered together a group of nonprofit leaders and asked about the tactics they employ to deal with mental stress, I have no doubt that many of the things I have discussed would surface, but many others would be added. Determine what works best for you. The main objective is to take a mental break.

When you experience stressful situations and you have a mental headache, give yourself a mental break. I know, firsthand, that if you do not give yourself a mental break, the health consequences can be devastating. Always place your health before the job. I know you want to continue helping others. I know the work is not complete. I know you cannot stop in the middle of a project. I know. I am telling you that you must take care of yourself to function well—and sometimes, to function at all. Your board, your staff, and the people you care for depend on you, but you must take a mental break and revitalize. Do it for them; do it for you.

11

Conclusion — The Fun-duh-mental Leader

YOU'RE HIRED, YOU NAVIGATE through the first days and weeks on the job, and you have proven that you are a nonprofit leader. You know the fundamental aspects of running a nonprofit organization. You understand the job duties, have built strong collaborations and relationships, have raised the necessary funds, and have developed a strong force of human resources. You created well-designed marketing materials and a standard operating procedures manual. Your business operations are running smoothly, and the organization is thriving.

As the leader, you know that the territory comes with daunting tasks, hard decisions, and challenging days, but you also know the power of felicity and how to have fun. You know when to take mental breaks, and you embrace the fact that you are human and, as such, cannot know and be everything to everyone. Nothing can stop you from reaching your goals and objectives. Nothing can stop you from building a sustainable organization that will be well respected throughout your community and ultimately the world.

You are truly the fun-duh-mental leader.

About the Author

RITA MCCOY, SERVED AS executive director of Sense of Security, a nonprofit organization that serves breast cancer patients who are struggling financially. She was responsible for fundraising, financials, operations, board development, program oversight, and staff management.

Rita worked as the community relations director at KTVD-TV for nearly ten years, and in that capacity, she worked closely with community and nonprofit leaders. She served on numerous committees and boards and served as board president of the Colorado Nonprofit Association and is an Honorary Trustee of the Women's Foundation of Colorado.

Rita McCoy is also an Emmy Award-winning television executive producer. She has held positions as executive director, adjunct professor, marketing and communication director, and television broadcasting and public relations professional.

Rita enjoys traveling with her husband, playing the piano, volunteering at local charities, attending networking socials, and spending time with her friends and family.

www.ingramcontent.com/pod-product-compliance
Lightning Source LLC
Chambersburg PA
CBHW022111210326
41521CB00028B/306